LAYING ON OF HANDS

Michael E.B. Maher

Unless otherwise indicated, all Scripture quotations in this teaching are from the *New King James Version* of the bible.

Revised Edition 2016

ISBN: 978-0-620-77669-1

Books by Michael E.B. Maher

Born Free from Sin
Repentance from Dead Works
Faith Towards God
Doctrine of Baptisms
Resurrection of the Dead
Eternal Judgement
The Will of Man
The Spirit of Man
The Conscience of Man
The Mind of Man
The Body of Man
Spiritual Gifts
The Revelation Gifts
The Power Gifts
Ministry Gifts
There is Sin to Death
Prayer
Of Such is the Kingdom
Overcoming Unforgiveness
Being led by the Spirit
The Two Gospels Explained

Contents

Chapter 1
What is the laying on of hands?

Introduction

Hebrews 5:12-14 "For though by this time you ought to be teachers, you need someone to teach you again the first principles of the oracles of God; and you have come to need milk and not solid food. (13) For everyone who partakes only of milk is unskilled in the word of righteousness, for he is a babe. (14) But solid food belongs to those who are of full age, that is, those who by reason of use have their senses exercised to discern both good and evil."

Hebrews 6:1-2 "Therefore, leaving the discussion of the elementary principles of Christ, let us go on to perfection, not laying again the foundation of repentance from dead works and of faith toward God, (2) of the doctrine of baptisms, of laying on of hands, of resurrection of the dead, and of eternal judgment."

There are six foundational doctrines to the Christian faith. Because they are foundational, every believer should have a clear understanding of each one of these doctrines, and live by them. Those who have a clear understanding of these doctrines and who also live by them, will have a sure foundation. And they will not be deceived by any false teachings, that they may come across in their Christian walk. Scripture reveals to us that these doctrines are the milk of God's word, which all new

What is the laying on of hands?

born believers should feed on. However, even mature adults drink milk as part of their natural diet. In the spirit, that principle remains the same. And so, it is good for mature believers to also revisit the foundational principles of Christ from time to time, to ensure that their foundations remain solid. In this teaching, we will examine the doctrine of the laying on of hands, which is the fourth of the six foundational doctrines taught to the body of Christ.

Jesus is our example

Mark 1:30-31 "But Simon's wife's mother lay sick with a fever, and they told Him about her at once. (31) So, He came and took her by the hand and lifted her up, and immediately the fever left her. And she served them."

Luke 4:38-41 "Now He arose from the synagogue and entered Simon's house. But Simon's wife's mother was sick with a high fever, and they made request of Him concerning her. (39) So, He stood over her and rebuked the fever, and it left her. And immediately she arose and served them. (40) When the sun was setting, all those who had any that were sick with various diseases brought them to Him; and He laid His hands on every one of them and healed them. (41) And demons also came out of many, crying out and saying, "You are the Christ, the Son of God!" And He, rebuking them, did not allow them to speak, for they knew that He was the Christ."

What is the laying on of hands?

It is our Lord Jesus, the head of the church, who has instructed us as His disciples, to lay our hands on people. For in the great commission, Jesus told us that those who believe in Him would lay their hands on the sick, and that the sick would recover. So, it would benefit us to look at how Jesus practised this ministry, so that we can learn from Him. Firstly, let me say that it is with the ministry of Jesus that we see, for the first time in the bible, the extensive use of this method of ministry. The examples that we see in the Old Testament are relatively few, in comparison to the New Testament. In the above account in Luke's gospel, we see Jesus laying His hands on those who were sick and healing them. Notice that the scripture tells us that Jesus laid His hands on every one of them. Our Lord also used the same method to cast out demons, for He was not only healing the sick that night, but He was also casting out demons. When our Lord laid His hands on people to heal them or to cast out demons, He always spoke to that sickness or demon at the same time. In speaking to the sickness or demon, He would rebuke it and command it to leave the individual that He was ministering to. In Mark's account quoted above, we see our Lord ministering healing to Peter's mother-in-law, through the laying on of hands. If we read only Mark's account of this incident, it seems to indicate that all that Jesus did was take her by the hand, and that was sufficient for her healing to take place. But that is not the case at all. Because when we look at Luke's account of the same incident, we see that in order to impart His healing power to her, Jesus did more than just take her hand in His. Luke's account in scripture, reveals to us that our Lord also rebuked the fever at the same time. And so, we see that in order to heal an individual and get them delivered, our Lord would lay His hands on that

What is the laying on of hands?

individual, and at the same time, He would rebuke whatever sickness or demon He may have been dealing with. Jesus would rebuke the sickness or demon, by commanding it to leave the body He was ministering to. Something else that we can see from this account, is that our Lord took Peter's mother-in-law by the hand when He rebuked the fever. In other words, He didn't lay His hands on her head to impart God's healing power. His hand holding her hand, had the same effect of transferring God's healing, as if He had laid hands on her head. The reason our Lord could do this in this instance, was because the fever was in her entire body. And so, His hands just touching her hands, had the effect of imparting God's healing power to her body to drive out the fever. Normally our Lord Jesus would place His hands on the affected part of the person's body, in order to heal that person's affliction. For example, when our Lord laid hands on those who were blind, He would place His hands on their eyes. And so, in following our Lord's example. When we lay hands on people, we are to lay our hands on the afflicted part of their bodies, and we are to rebuke whatever sickness we are dealing with and command it to leave that body in the name of Jesus.

Matthew 14:35-36 "And when the men of that place recognized Him, they sent out into all that surrounding region, brought to Him all who were sick, (36) and begged Him that they might only touch the hem of His garment. And as many as touched it were made perfectly well."

Luke 6:19 "And the whole multitude sought to touch Him, for power went out from Him and healed them all."

What is the laying on of hands?

Acts 10:38 "how God anointed Jesus of Nazareth with the Holy Spirit and with power, who went about doing good and healing all who were oppressed by the devil, for God was with Him."

When Jesus ministered on the earth, He ministered as a man anointed by the Holy Spirit to do the works of God. You will recall that when our Lord was baptized in water by John the Baptist, that God the Father then filled Him with the Holy Spirit. Prior to our Lord being filled with the Holy Spirit, He performed no miracles on the earth. And no demons recognised Him for who He was. It was only after our Lord was filled with the Spirit and anointed with power, that He began to minister healing and deliverance to the people. And it was only from that time onwards, that the demons recognised Him for the first time, and began to cry out whenever they came into His presence. So just why did our Lord Jesus lay His hands on people to heal them, and to cast out demons? The reason Jesus would lay His hands on people, was because primarily, the healing anointing was in His hands. I said that primarily the anointing was in our Lord's hands, but we can clearly see in the above account in scripture, when our Lord came into the region of Gennesaret, that all that the sick needed to do in order to be healed, was to touch His garments. The reason for this was because our Lord was so anointed, that even His clothes carried that anointing. Our Lord Jesus is the perfect example, because there was nothing in His life that hindered God's power from flowing through Him. And so, God's power rested on Him to such a degree, that even His clothes were anointed. The apostles, for a brief period when the church began, walked in that degree of

What is the laying on of hands?

anointing. To the point that even Peter's shadow falling on a sick person, would get them healed. But then divisions arose in the church, and that degree of anointing was lifted from the church. We can learn a very important lesson from this. In that we see that God the Father does not limit His power through us, we do. Jesus never limited God's power, and so He carried God's full anointing on Him. To the point, that anyone that just touched His clothes in faith, could receive God's healing power. In following our Lord's example, keep sin out of your life so that when you lay hands on others, there is nothing in you that can hinder the flow of God's power through you. The power that went out from our Lord Jesus was tangible, which is why people sought to just touch Him. The moment they touched Him in faith, they could feel that healing power flow into their bodies and they were healed.

Mark 5:29-30 "Immediately the fountain of her blood was dried up, and she felt in her body that she was healed of the affliction. (30) And Jesus, immediately knowing in Himself that power had gone out of Him, turned around in the crowd and said, "Who touched My clothes?"

Matthew 8:13 "Then Jesus said to the centurion, "Go your way; and as you have believed, so let it be done for you." And his servant was healed that same hour."

Mark's gospel quoted above, records the incident of the woman with the issue of blood, who was made well by only touching the Lord's garment. We know that she was healed by the anointing, for our Lord Jesus recognised that power, or the anointing, had gone out from Him.

What is the laying on of hands?

Once again, we see that Jesus was so saturated with the power of the Holy Spirit, that even His clothes carried that anointing while He was wearing them. Nevertheless, Jesus primary method of healing people, was to lay His hands on them. Just as power went out from Him through His clothes when the woman with the issue of blood touched Him, so power or the anointing went out from Him though His hands, into the bodies of whomever He was healing at the time. The anointing on Jesus was a tangible power that could be felt, as it flowed from His hands into the bodies of those needing healing. The woman with the issue of blood, felt that power flow into her body when she was healed. Although laying on of hands was the primary way that Jesus ministered to the sick, as we have already seen, it was not the only way He ministered. Our Lord also healed simply by speaking words of faith. In the above account in Matthew's gospel, our Lord Jesus did not lay hands on the centurion's servant. He simply spoke the word, and the centurion's servant was healed. There are many other ways recorded in scripture in which Jesus healed the sick, but we will not examine them in this teaching, because the focus of this teaching is the laying on of hands.

Mark 8:22-26 "Then He came to Bethsaida; and they brought a blind man to Him, and begged Him to touch him. (23) So, He took the blind man by the hand and led him out of the town. And when He had spit on his eyes and put His hands on him, He asked him if he saw anything. (24) And he looked up and said, "I see men like trees, walking." (25) Then He put His hands on his eyes again and made him look up. And he was restored and saw everyone clearly. (26) Then He sent him away to his house,

What is the laying on of hands?

saying, "Neither go into the town, nor tell anyone in the town."

When we look at our Lord's ministry, we sometimes mistakenly think that everyone our Lord laid hands on, was instantly healed. But that is not the case. Because even though the Lord Jesus was saturated with God's healing power, it still required faith on the part of the person needing healing, to receive that anointing. When Jesus laid His hands on people, not always did those people instantly receive their healing or deliverance. There were occasions when our Lord had to take His time, to get people healed and delivered. In the above account, we see our Lord taking quite a bit of time to get this blind man healed. So, what was different on this occasion, which prevented the man from receiving his healing instantly from Jesus, as we saw earlier when all who just touched His garment were made perfectly well? The answer is unbelief. When they brought the blind man to Jesus, our Lord was reluctant to lay hands on him, because He perceived that the man's faith was not very strong. Which is why they had to beg Jesus to lay hands on him. Also, there were many spectators there, who were also in unbelief. When unbelief is present, it hinders the flow of God's power from being manifested. And so, our Lord had to take the man away from the midst of all the spectators, and lead him out of the town. When Jesus led the man out of the town He instructed His disciples to prevent the people from following Him. How do we know that? You will recall the time that our Lord raised the little girl from the dead, that there was a whole crowd following Him. But scripture tells us that Jesus only allowed Peter, James and John to go with Him. How did He do that? He instructed His disciples to prevent anyone from following

What is the laying on of hands?

Him to the little girl's house. We know that no one in the town of Bethsaida witnessed this particular miracle taking place. Because after Jesus healed the man, our Lord instructed him not to tell anyone in the town, *"Neither go into the town, nor tell anyone in the town"*. Not only did our Lord have to deal with the unbelief of the spectators, but He also had to deal with the weak faith in the blind man as well. Which is why our Lord had to do something more than just lay hands on the man. The account tells us that our Lord, in this instance, also spat on the man's eyes. This man needed some help in releasing his faith. And just as pouring oil on the sick at times, helps them to release their faith as they feel the oil on their bodies, so feeling the Lord's spittle on his eyes, helped this man release his faith to receive God's healing power. But even though our Lord did as much as He could to get the man to release his faith, initially the man only received partial healing. And so, our Lord had to lay hands on him a second time, and this time he received his full healing. If it was up to the Lord alone, this man would have been instantly healed. But it wasn't up to the Lord alone. The blind man's faith was involved. And that is why it took the Lord some time to heal him. Remember, that in this section we are looking at our Lord Jesus ministry of laying on of hands, to learn from Him how to do this. Most believers encountering a similar situation as we have read in this passage, would have simply laid hands on the blind man when asked to do so. And nothing would have happened. In order to get results, first discern the level of faith in the person you are laying hands on. Secondly, make sure the person is out of an environment where unbelief is present. Thirdly, follow the leading of the Holy Spirit if He is wanting you to do something extra to activate the person's faith. And then finally, if only a

What is the laying on of hands?

partial manifestation of healing occurs when hands are laid initially, then lay hands on the individual a second time.

Mark 5:1-13 "Then they came to the other side of the sea, to the country of the Gadarenes. (2) And when He had come out of the boat, immediately there met Him out of the tombs a man with an unclean spirit, ... (6) When he saw Jesus from afar, he ran and worshiped Him. (7) And he cried out with a loud voice and said, "What have I to do with You, Jesus, Son of the Most High God? I implore You by God that You do not torment me." (8) For He said to him, "Come out of the man, unclean spirit!" (9) Then He asked him, "What is your name?" And he answered, saying, "My name is Legion; for we are many." (10) Also, he begged Him earnestly that He would not send them out of the country. (11) Now a large herd of swine was feeding there near the mountains. (12) So, all the demons begged Him, saying, "Send us to the swine, that we may enter them." (13) And at once Jesus gave them permission. Then the unclean spirits went out and entered the swine (there were about two thousand); and the herd ran violently down the steep place into the sea, and drowned in the sea."

When Jesus cast demons out of people, not always did the demons leave straight away. In this account that we have just read, it took our Lord a bit of time to get the demons cast out of this man. If we examine the sequence of events as they happened, we can see that it took the Lord a bit of time to cast these demons out. The account starts when the demon possessed man, ran up to Jesus to worship Him. The reason he did that, was because the demon recognized Jesus for who He was. In scripture, we see that after our Lord was baptized with the Holy Spirit, that all demons could then recognize Him for who He was. It was when the demon began to worship Jesus, that our Lord then commanded the demon to come out of the man. But even though our Lord had commanded the demon to come out of the man, the demon did not leave, but instead spoke back to the Lord. For the scripture tells us that the demon then cried out with a loud voice, *"And he cried out with a loud voice and said, "What have I to do with You, Jesus, Son of the Most High God? I implore You by God that You do not torment me."* It was at this stage that our Lord then asked the demon what his name was, and the demon gave his name. The demon then asked the Lord not to send him out of the country. Luke's account of this incident tells us that the demon begged not to be cast into the Abyss. Up until this point, the demon whose name was Legion, had been using the man's voice to speak to Jesus. For it was that demon that had possessed the man, and so had control of the man's voice. Then we see something else take place, which took place in the realm of the spirit. The bible teaches us that all the demons then began to beg Jesus to let them go into the swine. Only Jesus could hear the approximately two thousand demons begging Him at this stage. Jesus then gave them permission, and they came out of the man. The point that I wanted to make from this account, is that it took our Lord a bit of time to get this man delivered. And so, if there were instances where it took our Lord a bit longer to get people healed and delivered, then we can expect that there will be times when it will also take us some time to get people healed and delivered. The key is to be led by the Spirit when laying hands on people, and also follow after the examples given to us in scripture, such as the one we have just read.

Hebrews 2:17 "Therefore, in all things He had to be made like His brethren, that He might be a merciful and faithful High Priest in things pertaining to God, to make propitiation for the sins of the people."

Psalms 35:13-14 "But as for me, when they were sick, My clothing was sackcloth; I humbled myself with fasting; And my prayer would return to my own heart. (14) I paced about as though he were my friend or brother; I bowed down heavily, as one who mourns for his mother."

We look at the life of our Lord Jesus in the gospel accounts, and we see Him being used of God to perform many miracles and healings, and even though we know that He walked this earth as a man, we think that somehow, He could do what He did, because He was special. Well, He was special. Our Lord Jesus walked this life in the flesh, without ever once committing any sin. But what we fail to realize, is that Jesus had to walk this life as we do. For scripture tells us that our Lord had to be made in all things, just like us. The point that I need you to see here, is that the anointing that was manifested through Jesus when He walked the earth, was not because of Him being the Son of God. The account in Psalms that I have quoted above, is an account of the private prayer life of our Lord Jesus, when He walked in the flesh. More specifically, we see how our Lord interceded to the Father on behalf of the sick, so that He would be used of God to heal them through His ministry. In this account, we see

What is the laying on of hands?

that not only did our Lord pray for the sick, but He also humbled Himself, in fasting for them. It was because of our Lord's intercessory prayer life, that God the Father anointed Jesus with the degree of healing power that He walked in. Our Lord Jesus said that we would do the same works that He did, and even greater works because He was going to the Father. If we are going to experience similar results as our Lord when we lay hands on people, then we are going to have to follow His example in every way, including our prayer lives. Prayer and fasting has the effect of increases the anointing in our lives. In the same manner, lack of prayer and fasting will diminish the anointing in our lives.

There are different anointing's

Acts 8:5-8 "Then Philip went down to the city of Samaria and preached Christ to them. (6) And the multitudes with one accord heeded the things spoken by Philip, hearing and seeing the miracles which he did. (7) For unclean spirits, crying with a loud voice, came out of many who were possessed; and many who were paralyzed and lame were healed. (8) And there was great joy in that city."

1 Corinthians 12:4-11 "There are diversities of gifts, but the same Spirit. (5) There are differences of ministries, but the same Lord. (6) And there are diversities of activities, but it is the same God who works all in all. (7) But the manifestation of the Spirit is given to each one for the profit of all: (8) for to one is given the word of wisdom through the Spirit, to another the word of knowledge through the same Spirit, (9) to another faith by the same Spirit,

What is the laying on of hands?

to another gifts of healings by the same Spirit, (10) to another the working of miracles, to another prophecy, to another discerning of spirits, to another different kinds of tongues, to another the interpretation of tongues. (11) But one and the same Spirit works all these things, distributing to each one individually as He wills."

Our Lord Jesus had all the gifts of the Spirit operating through His ministry. But that is not the case with us. We receive gifts from the Holy Spirit, as He wills. But each member in the body of Christ has received at least one gift. Ministering in the gifts of the Spirit, is what the doctrine of laying on of hands, is primarily all about. There are different types of anointing's. In the book of Corinthians quoted above, the Holy Spirit teaches us about His gifts. He lists nine gifts. Each gift carries a different type of anointing. But even within the various gifts, the Holy Spirit tells us that there are *"differences of ministries"* and *"diversities of activities"*. So, it is possible for two members of the body of Christ to have the same gift, but operate differently to each other in ministering that gift. For example, I have seen two prophets, both operate in the gift of the word of knowledge. While the one prophet could tell a person to simply stand up in the audience, and then minister the word of knowledge to them. The other prophet had to have the person come stand in front of them and then lay hands on them, and only then were they able to minister the word of knowledge to them. In both cases, it was the gift of the word of knowledge being manifested, but there was a difference in the way they ministered that gift. The gifts of healings would be another example. Notice that it is called gifts (plural) of healings (plural). For example, some are

What is the laying on of hands?

anointed to heal blindness, while others are anointed to heal people who are paralyzed. In the above account from the book of Acts, we see Philip being used to heal many paralyzed and lame people. I'm sure that there were blind and deaf people in the crowds at Philip's meetings, but the bible mentions nothing about them being healed. The reason for this is because Philip was not anointed in that area. When it comes to us laying hands on people to minister to them, it is very important that we know firstly, what our gifting's are. And then secondly, how or what method, the Holy Spirit wants us to use, in ministering the gifts that He has given us. When we do this, we will see greater results in our laying on of hands. We will also see that we will be able to more easily release our faith, in the operation of our gifts. For each one of us receives ministry gift faith, according to the measure of the gift that we have received from Him.

Faith is required

Mark 6:5-6 "Now He could do no mighty work there, except that He laid His hands on a few sick people and healed them. (6) And He marveled because of their unbelief. Then He went about the villages in a circuit, teaching."

2 Corinthians 4:7 "But we have this treasure in earthen vessels, that the excellence of the power may be of God and not of us."

In all instances when the saints are used by God to lay hands on people, it is so that His anointing and His power can be imparted to that individual. The laying on of hands is all about the impartation of God's anointing, power and blessing. But I want you to note, that faith is always involved. The simple act of one person laying their hands on another individual has absolutely no effect whatsoever, if that act is not done in faith. For it is God's power. No human has any inherit power of their own, that they can impart to another individual. Our bodies are nothing but the vessels that God uses, to impart His power to others. The apostle Paul was mightily used of the Lord through the laying on of hands to heal the sick, to fill the saints with the Holy Spirit, and even to raise the dead. But in all of that, he acknowledged that it was God's power, and that he was just the vessel of the Lord that carried His power. If faith were not involved, then the simple act of laying on of hands, would always get one hundred percent results. But we know that is not the case. The reason for that is because the laying on of hands works by faith, and faith alone. If faith were not required to ensure that God's power is transferred through the laying on of hands, then the Son of God could have ensured that the Father's power would have been transferred through the laying on of His hands, in His hometown of Nazareth. But as scripture reveals to us, even Jesus was not able to impart God's power through the laying on of His hands, if the individuals He ministered to, refused to believe. The people in Jesus home town couldn't accept the fact that this person who had grown up among them, was an anointed prophet of God. Their unbelief prevented Jesus from performing any mighty miracle that He had been able to perform in all the other surrounding towns. The laying on of hands acts as a point of contact, whereby the person can release their faith to receive from God. The act of laying on of hands however, requires faith from both the one receiving from God, and from the one who is doing the laying on of hands. In the above passage of scripture from Mark's gospel, our Lord Jesus had faith in the anointing of God that was upon Him, and He was ready to release God's power through the laying on of His hands. But in His hometown of Nazareth, there were not many who had the faith to receive God's power through Him, because they simply just didn't believe. And our Lord Jesus marveled at their unbelief. In fact, unbelief is the biggest hindrance to the power of God being made manifest through the laying on of hands. I have experienced instances when the power of God has been so strong in my hands (it's as if raw electricity is flowing through them), that I cannot close them. And yet on those occasions, when I have laid hands on some individuals who have asked for prayer for healing, nothing happened. I could fell that no transference of power took place. What was the reason? Simple unbelief.

2 Kings 2:9-10 "And so it was, when they had crossed over, that Elijah said to Elisha, "Ask! What may I do for you, before I am taken away from you?" Elisha said, "Please let a double portion of your spirit be upon me." (10) So, he said, "You have asked a hard thing. Nevertheless, if you see me when I am taken from you, it shall be so for you; but if not, it shall not be so."

2 Kings 13:20-21 "Then Elisha died, and they buried him. And the raiding bands from Moab invaded the land in the spring of the year. (21) So, it was, as they were burying a man, that suddenly they spied a band of raiders; and they put the man in the tomb of Elisha; and when the man was let down and

What is the laying on of hands?

touched the bones of Elisha, he revived and stood on his feet."

The anointing or power of God, is very real. Elisha was a prophet of God who was mightily anointed by God. In fact, as we have seen in the above passage of scripture, he carried a double portion of Elijah's anointing. If you study the lives of both these men, you will see that they were mightily used of the Lord in demonstrating God's power, through the gifts of the Spirit. And the recorded miracles performed through Elisha's ministry was double that recorded in Elijah's ministry. The second account of scripture quoted above, shows us just how real the anointing of God is. The background to this account is that Elisha had died, and had been buried in a tomb. Because of the passing of time, his body had decayed to the point that only his bones remained in the tomb. However, after all that time, a residue of the anointing of God that was on him during his lifetime, was still in his bones. When a certain dead man was lowered into Elisha's tomb because of a hasty burial, the moment the dead man's body touched the bones of Elisha, the dead man came back to life. In this case, no-one's faith was involved. For Elisha wasn't there, only his bones. And the dead man certainly wasn't exercising his faith. And neither were the folks who were burying him, expecting to see their friend being raised from the dead. The only thing present, that was still residing in Elisha's bones after all that time, was the anointing of God. God's anointing is very real. God's power and anointing are one and the same thing. And so, we see that the doctrine of laying on of hands is a doctrine of the impartation of God's power. But again, I must emphasize that without faith, the act of laying on of hands becomes nothing more than a religious practice. Also, faith must be released by both parties involved, i.e. the person laying hands and the person upon whom hands are being laid, if the impartation of God's power is to take place.

The anointing is in our hands

Romans 6:18 "And having been set free from sin, you became slaves of righteousness."

1 Corinthians 6:19-20 "Or do you not know that your body is the temple of the Holy Spirit who is in you, whom you have from God, and you are not your own? (20) For you were bought at a price; therefore, glorify God in your body and in your spirit, which are God's."

So why do we lay hands on people? Other than the fact that it is more practical to lay hands on people, than any other part of our bodies, the anointing to minister resides in our hands. Many of those anointed to minister to the sick speak of a burning sensation in their hands, when the anointing comes on them to minister. I know in my own case, that the power of God feels as if raw electricity is flowing through my hands. It is not only for ministering to the sick, that we use our hands however. You will recall that I mentioned earlier that I witnessed a prophet only being able to minister the word of knowledge, through the laying on of hands. He is not the only one, as many other prophets experience the same thing. Their gift will not work unless they lay hands on the individual. Very often, the Holy Spirit uses the laying on of hands to activate the gift in the individual using that gift. Residing on the inside of each one of His saints is the

What is the laying on of hands?

blessed Holy Spirit, for we are the temple of the Holy Spirit. The reason that we are the temple of the Holy Spirit is because under the New Covenant, our spirits are born again, and are completely free from all sin. Because the is no sin in our spirits, the Holy Spirit can now reside in our spirits. Because our spirits reside in our earthly bodies, the Holy Spirit resides in our earthly bodies also. Therefore, the Holy Spirit, in writing through the apostle Paul, tells us that our bodies have become His temple. I want you to notice that the Holy Spirit tells us that not only do our spirits belong to Him, but our bodies belong to Him also. The reason our bodies belong to Him, is because they have been paid for by the precious blood of the Lamb. And so, the reason that we lay hands on others is because ultimately, our hands are His hands. And as such, God Himself desires to use our hands to impart His blessing to others around us.

Oil can be used

Mark 6:7-13 "And He called the twelve to Himself, and began to send them out two by two, and gave them power over unclean spirits. ... (12) So they went out and preached that people should repent. (13) And they cast out many demons, and anointed with oil many who were sick, and healed them."

James 5:14-15 "Is anyone among you sick? Let him call for the elders of the church, and let them pray over him, anointing him with oil in the name of the Lord. (15) And the prayer of faith will save the sick, and the Lord will raise him up. And if he has committed sins, he will be forgiven."

What is the laying on of hands?

Oil in scripture, is a type of the anointing of the Holy Spirit. There are number of things that we can learn from these portions of scripture, regarding the ministry of laying on of hands. Firstly, although scripture does not specifically state it, the above scripture from Mark's gospel, reveals to us that our Lord Jesus also healed the sick through the anointing of oil. Before our Lord Jesus sent His disciples out to minister healing to the sick, He taught them how to do it. The scripture tells us that the disciples, *"anointed with oil many who were sick, and healed them."* They did that, because Jesus told them to do it, and He also showed them how to do it. There is something else we can learn from the portion of scripture in Mark's gospel, regarding the impartation of God's power. The scripture tells us that our Lord gave the disciples power. How did He do that? He did that, by laying His hands on them, and imparting the same anointing that was on Him, into their hands. The disciples would have felt the tangible power of God flow from Jesus, into their hands. Kenneth E. Hagin, in recounting a similar experience that he had when our Lord appeared to him, tells of the Lord Jesus placing His finger in the palms of each one of his hands. And the moment our Lord did that, Kenneth's hands began to have a burning sensation in them. But the main thing I wanted to comment on from these portions of scripture, is that oil is also used as a mechanism, to heal the sick. There were no special healing properties in the oil that the disciples used, which caused the healing to take place in the sick. As with our hands, when oil is poured on an individual to receive their healing, it is used purely as a point of contact whereby the person being prayed for, can release their faith to receive their healing. Many times, not always, when people experience the tangible healing power of God entering their bodies, it feels like a warmth coming over them. Oil, in the natural, has a similar feeling, in that it flows over the individual. Oil is used in the natural, to help people to release their faith in the spirit. In the second portion of scripture quoted above, the Holy Spirit through James the apostle, tells the elders of the church to anoint the sick with oil, when they pray for them. But notice that it is still the prayer of faith that heals the sick, not the oil. Again, the oil is used purely as an aid for the person to be able to release their faith, and thus be healed.

There is a transference of anointing

Acts 2:1-4 "When the Day of Pentecost had fully come, they were all with one accord in one place. (2) And suddenly there came a sound from heaven, as of a rushing mighty wind, and it filled the whole house where they were sitting. (3) Then there appeared to them divided tongues, as of fire, and one sat upon each of them. (4) And they were all filled with the Holy Spirit and began to speak with other tongues, as the Spirit gave them utterance."

Acts 8:14-17 "Now when the apostles who were at Jerusalem heard that Samaria had received the word of God, they sent Peter and John to them, (15) who, when they had come down, prayed for them that they might receive the Holy Spirit. (16) For as yet He had fallen upon none of them. They had only been baptized in the name of the Lord Jesus. (17) Then they laid hands on them, and they received the Holy Spirit."

What is the laying on of hands?

This brings us to a very important point, and that is the transference of God's anointing or His power, if you will. Very often the impartation of God's ability and His power, is done through physical contact. This is not always the case, because we have seen in scripture where the Lord imparted His blessing to people, directly from heaven. In the first passage of scripture quoted above, our Lord Jesus received the promise of the Holy Spirit from the Father, and He poured out the Holy Spirit from heaven, directly onto His saints. But in the next quoted account in scripture, we have record of the saints in Samaria, being filled with the Holy Spirit for the first time, via a different method. We see that they were filled with the Holy Spirit, through the laying on of the apostle's hands. In other words, the anointing of the Holy Spirit that was on the inside of Peter and John, flowed through their hands into the saints for which they had prayed.

Luke 22:43 "Then an angel appeared to Him from heaven, strengthening Him."

Daniel 10:16-19 "And suddenly, one having the likeness of the sons of men touched my lips; then I opened my mouth and spoke, saying to him who stood before me, "My lord, because of the vision my sorrows have overwhelmed me, and I have retained no strength. (17) For how can this servant of my lord talk with you, my lord? As for me, no strength remains in me now, nor is any breath left in me." (18) Then again, the one having the likeness of a man touched me and strengthened me. (19) And he said, "O man greatly beloved, fear not! Peace be to you; be strong, yes, be strong!" So, when he spoke to

What is the laying on of hands?

me I was strengthened, and said, "Let my lord speak, for you have strengthened me."

God uses His angels in the same manner, for they too impart His power through the laying on of their hands. The above passage of scripture speaks of the account in the garden of Gethsemane when our Lord was praying, as He was about to undergo the suffering on the cross. At that time God the Father sent an angel to Him, who when he had come, placed his hands on Jesus, and strengthened Him. You say, I can see that the angel strengthened our Lord, but how do you know that he did so through the laying on of his hands? We know that the angel strengthened our Lord through the laying on of hands, because in the next account of scripture quoted above, the angel Gabriel did exactly that. In this account, the angel Gabriel had appeared to the prophet Daniel, in a vision. Because of the power of the vision, Daniel's physical body could not stand it and he became extremely weak. The angel Gabriel stretched out his hand and touched Daniel and spoke words of strength into Daniel, thus imparting strength to him.

Acts 28:8 "And it happened that the father of Publius lay sick of a fever and dysentery. Paul went in to him and prayed, and he laid his hands on him and healed him."

Acts 19:11-12 "Now God worked unusual miracles by the hands of Paul, (12) so that even handkerchiefs or aprons were brought from his body to the sick, and the diseases left them and the evil spirits went out of them."

What is the laying on of hands?

Paul prayed for people to be healed through the transference of the healing anointing, as he laid hands on them. In the above account, Paul prayed for an unsaved man to be healed and at the same time he laid his hands on the man. The result was that God's healing power went out of Paul's hands into the man, and he was healed. We know that the healing anointing operated through Paul's ministry, because it was the anointing that went out of his hands into the aprons that were used to heal the sick. When Paul prayed, and laid his hands on those handkerchiefs and aprons, the anointing would flow out of his hands and be stored in those cloths. When those cloths in turn were laid on those needing healing, if they had faith, then that anointing would be released into their bodies and effect their healing. Remember we read where Jesus clothes also carried His healing anointing, so that any who touched His garments were healed.

Greater anointing's have greater results

John 3:34 "For He whom God has sent speaks the words of God, for God does not give the Spirit by measure."

Ephesians 4:7 "But to each one of us grace was given according to the measure of Christ's gift."

This brings us to another important point, and that is the degree of anointing or measure of God's power that resides in each one of us. As we can see from the passage of scripture in Ephesians, every saint carries a measure of God's power or anointing within their spirits. But not every saint has the same measure of God's power, residing inside of them. The Holy Spirit speaking through John the

Baptist, tells us in John's gospel, that God gave to Jesus of Nazareth, the Spirit without measure. In other words, Jesus carried within Him the full measure of God's power, when He walked the earth. By implication, the Holy Spirit is telling us that we carry the power of the Holy Spirit, by measure. In other words, we don't carry the full anointing of the Holy Spirit in us, as Jesus did. This agrees with what the apostle Paul has written to the church. For Paul tells us that each of us have received grace, or God's anointing, according to the measure of the gift that each of us have received from the Lord. Some have received the gift of the apostle while others have received the gift of prophecy. You can readily understand that the gift of apostle requires a greater anointing to be able to function in that gift, compared to the degree of anointing required to operate in the simple gift of prophecy. I have quoted these two gifts purely to illustrate the point that certain gifts require more anointing or power, than others do. As we look at the different areas in this teaching where we as believers, lay hands on people, this point becomes important to keep in mind. Because just as we can all lay hands on others simply in faith, the transference of anointing takes place that much more effectively when someone is specifically anointed in that area. Let me illustrate this point by means of an example given to us scripture.

Acts 8:5-17 "Then Philip went down to the city of Samaria and preached Christ to them. (6) And the multitudes with one accord heeded the things spoken by Philip, hearing and seeing the miracles which he did. (7) For unclean spirits, crying with a loud voice, came out of many who were possessed; and many who were paralyzed and lame were healed. (8) And there was great joy in that city. ... (14) Now when the apostles who were at Jerusalem heard that Samaria had received the word of God, they sent Peter and John to them, (15) who, when they had come down, prayed for them that they might receive the Holy Spirit. (16) For as yet He had fallen upon none of them. They had only been baptized in the name of the Lord Jesus. (17) Then they laid hands on them, and they received the Holy Spirit."

Romans 12:3-5 "For I say, through the grace given to me, to everyone who is among you, not to think of himself more highly than he ought to think, but to think soberly, as God has dealt to each one a measure of faith. (4) For as we have many members in one body, but all the members do not have the same function, (5) so we, being many, are one body in Christ, and individually members of one another."

When persecution against the church in Jerusalem occurred after Stephen was martyred, the saints were scattered and went everywhere preaching the gospel. Philip, who was one of the seven, went down to the city of Samaria where he preached the gospel. Scripture reveals to us that he had a city-wide revival, and that multitudes responded to his message by giving their hearts to the Lord. Not only were many saved through his ministry, but also many were healed and delivered through his laying on of hands. When Philip ministered in Samaria, many were saved, healed and delivered, but as we read further in that account we see that no one was filled with the Holy Spirit. So why is that? Philip had no problem laying hands on many who were sick and demon possessed, so why not lay hands on them to get them filled with the Spirit? The reason was because Philip had received the spiritual gift of healings from the Lord, and thus he carried the anointing to be able to minister God's power to the multitudes, in healing and deliverance. But when it came to laying hands on believers to be filled with the Holy Spirit, Philip recognized that he was not anointed in that area, because that wasn't his gift. For the ministry of the laying on of hands for the infilling of the Holy Spirit, is also a gift from the Lord, and carries a different anointing. And so, Philip asked the church in Jerusalem to send him help in that area. In response to Philip's request, the church in Jerusalem specifically sent the apostles, Peter and John to Samaria to lay hands on the saints. The reason they did that, was because Peter and John had received the ministry gift from the Lord for the infilling of the Holy Spirit, and they were therefore anointed in that area. Philip could certainly have laid hands on each one in faith, and prayed for them to be filled with the Holy Spirit. But scripture tells us that multitudes were saved. And for Philip to pray in faith for each one in turn, to receive the infilling of the Spirit would not have been nearly as effective as having people pray, who were specifically anointed by the Lord to minister in that area. Philip recognized that he couldn't do it all, and that each one of us have received our own gift from the Lord. And we are to walk in our callings and defer to others in the body of Christ, in areas where we have not received those gifts from the Lord. In the above passage of scripture from the book of Romans, the Holy Spirit through the apostle Paul, reinforces this truth by telling us not to think of ourselves more highly than we ought to think. But we are to recognize that we are part of the body of Christ and each one of us have their own roles to fill. And that each of us have received different anointing's from the Lord.

Chapter 2
Laying hands on the unsaved

We lay hands to fulfil the great commission

Acts 3:6-8 "Then Peter said, "Silver and gold I do not have, but what I do have I give you: In the name of Jesus Christ of Nazareth, rise up and walk." (7) And he took him by the right hand and lifted him up, and immediately his feet and ankle bones received strength. (8) So he, leaping up, stood and walked and entered the temple with them--walking, leaping, and praising God."

Acts 5:12-16 "And through the hands of the apostles many signs and wonders were done among the people. ... (15) so that they brought the sick out into the streets and laid them on beds and couches, that at least the shadow of Peter passing by might fall on some of them. (16) Also a multitude gathered from the surrounding cities to Jerusalem, bringing sick people and those who were tormented by unclean spirits, and they were all healed."

Acts 8:5-7 "Then Philip went down to the city of Samaria and preached Christ to them. (6) And the multitudes with one accord heeded the things spoken by Philip, hearing and seeing the miracles which he did. (7) For unclean spirits, crying with a loud voice, came out of many who were possessed; and many who were paralyzed and lame were healed."

Laying hands on the unsaved

Acts 9:32-34 "Now it came to pass, as Peter went through all parts of the country, that he also came down to the saints who dwelt in Lydda. (33) There he found a certain man named Aeneas, who had been bedridden eight years and was paralyzed. (34) And Peter said to him, "Aeneas, Jesus the Christ heals you. Arise and make your bed." Then he arose immediately."

Acts 14:8-10 "And in Lystra a certain man without strength in his feet was sitting, a cripple from his mother's womb, who had never walked. (9) This man heard Paul speaking. Paul, observing him intently and seeing that he had faith to be healed, (10) said with a loud voice, "Stand up straight on your feet!" And he leaped and walked."

Acts 28:8-9 "And it happened that the father of Publius lay sick of a fever and dysentery. Paul went in to him and prayed, and he laid his hands on him and healed him. (9) So when this was done, the rest of those on the island who had diseases also came and were healed."

In the book of Acts, there are only six accounts recorded, of specific healings taking place. I have listed those accounts in the scriptures quoted above. There are other accounts of inferences to healings, such as the Lord working special miracles through the hands of Paul, in that Paul laid his hands on cloths to heal people. But I am referring to specific accounts in scripture, of healings taking place. It is extremely significant that the Holy Spirit has recorded these accounts for us. Because besides the fact that each is an account of someone being healed, there is one other significant common denominator. Each account recorded, is of believers being used by the Lord, to heal the unsaved. By recording these accounts for us, the Holy Spirit is emphasizing to us, that the church's mandate is to lay their hands on the sick of the unsaved. You say, what about the sick of those who are saved? Well we will see later in this teaching that believers have a right to walk in divine health, and so should not need to have hands laid on them for healing. But the bible does however, make provision for hands to be laid on believers for healing, which we will look at in another chapter.

Mark 16:15-18 "And He said to them, "Go into all the world and preach the gospel to every creature. (16) He who believes and is baptized will be saved; but he who does not believe will be condemned. (17) And these signs will follow those who believe: In My name they will cast out demons; they will speak with new tongues; (18) they will take up serpents; and if they drink anything deadly, it will by no means hurt them; they will lay hands on the sick, and they will recover."

1 Corinthians 14:21-22 "In the law it is written: "WITH MEN OF OTHER TONGUES AND OTHER LIPS I WILL SPEAK TO THIS PEOPLE; AND YET, FOR ALL THAT, THEY WILL NOT HEAR ME," says the Lord. (22) Therefore, tongues are for a sign, not to those who believe but to unbelievers; but prophesying is not for unbelievers but for those who believe."

Laying hands on the unsaved

Romans 10:17 "So then faith comes by hearing, and hearing by the word of God."

So why do we say that our Lord Jesus has called each of His saints to lay hands on the unsaved? The bible teaches us that there are certain areas where the Lord Jesus expects all His saints to lay hands. He expects this of us, because He has enabled each one of us to do just that. We are all familiar with the above passage of scripture from Mark's gospel, in which our Lord Jesus gave us what is often referred to, as the "great commission". In this passage our Lord tells us what we, as His believers, are required to do. We are to go into all the world and preach the gospel to every creature. Now we know that He is not saying that every believer must become a full-time minister of the gospel. But rather He is saying is that every believer should witness to those around them, about their testimony of salvation through Jesus Christ our Lord. Our Lord then goes on to tell us, what signs will follow those who believe. In other words, these are the signs that He will perform, through those who believe. A key word used by the Lord in this passage of scripture, is the word "signs". Signs are always used by God, for the unsaved, not for believers. One of the signs that our Lord said would follow those who believe, is that they will speak with new tongues. In the above passage of scripture quoted from the book of Corinthians, the Holy Spirit through the apostle Paul, clearly tells us that tongues are for a sign to unbelievers. Two of the signs that our Lord mentioned in Mark's gospel, refers to His saints ministering to others. He said that those who believe, will cast out demons, and that they will lay their hands on the sick and that the sick would recover. In context, our Lord is telling us that this is how He wants us to minister to the unsaved. For these are the accompanying signs that He will perform, when we preach the gospel of salvation to the unsaved. And so, we see that as far as Jesus is concerned, the ministry of casting out demons and laying on of hands on the sick, is for every believer. In other words, just as Jesus expects every one of us to witness to the unsaved about Him, so He expects every one of us to cast out their demons and lay our hands on their sick so that they may recover. You say how can Jesus expect every believer to cast out demons and heal the sick? Well we all agree (at least every believer should agree) that our Lord Jesus expects all of us to witness to those around us, about salvation through Him. Now we all know that our Lord has called some to full time ministry, and given them a special anointing to preach the gospel to the unsaved. The evangelist Billy Graham, is an example of someone like that. But although the Lord's evangelists are mightily used by Him to add multitudes to the church, they are not going to reach everyone. There are unsaved people that you know, who have never heard Billy Graham preach the gospel, and most probably never will. But those same unsaved people, encounter you every day and they can see your changed lifestyle since you were saved. It is to those people that our Lord Jesus expects you, as His ambassador, to tell them about Him. I want you to notice that Jesus does not expect you to get them saved. You can't do that, only He can. Jesus only expects us to tell people about Him, and He then works the miracle of the new birth, in those who choose to believe.

And so, we come to laying hands on the sick to be healed and the casting out of demons. We also know that our Lord has raised up ministry gifts and given them a special anointing's, to minister His healing power to the sick and to cast out demons. Smith Wigglesworth would have been an example of just such a ministry. But again, unsaved people that you know who are ill, have most probably never heard of any ministers of the gospel that are specially anointed by the Lord, to heal the sick and cast out demons. And so, they will never experience receiving their healing through those ministries. But those same unsaved people who are ill, encounter you every day. It is those people that our Lord Jesus expects you to lay hands on. I want you to notice that Jesus does not expect you to get them healed and delivered. You can't do that, only He can. Jesus only expects us to pray in faith for those people, and lay our hands on them. And He then works the miracle of healing and deliverance, in those who choose to believe. For it is the same Holy Spirit that resides in every anointed minister of the gospel, who dwells in every believer. And ultimately, He is the healer. Believers who are obedient to tell the unsaved about salvation through Jesus Christ, will experience seeing some get saved. But just as not everyone is saved who hears an evangelist preach the gospel, not everyone that you witness to, will be saved. For not everyone will believe the gospel. Now just because some don't believe, we don't then stop telling others about the gospel of salvation through Jesus. No, our mandate is to tell people about Jesus, and so we continue telling them. In the same manner, believers who are obedient to lay hands on the sick and pray for them in the name of Jesus Christ, will experience seeing some get healed and delivered. But also, just as not everyone is healed who have an anointed minister lay hands on them, not everyone that you pray for will be healed. For not everyone will believe in the healing power of our Lord Jesus. But just because some don't receive healing when we pray, we don't then stop praying for others to be healed and delivered. No, our mandate is to lay hands on people in Jesus name, and so we continue praying for them. Notice that I said that not everyone will believe, in the healing power of Jesus. Scripture teaches us that faith comes by hearing, and hearing the word of God. No one witnesses to the unsaved, by walking up to them and asking them if they can pray for them to receive salvation through Jesus. People would think that they are nuts. We first witness to people, about salvation through Jesus. The Holy Spirit then takes those words to minister to them, so that their faith can be stirred up to respond to the message of salvation. For the scripture quoted from the book of Romans above, tells us that faith comes by hearing and hearing by the word of God. And so, it is only after we have witnessed to the unsaved, that we ask them if we can pray with them to be saved. In the same manner when we pray for the unsaved to be healed and delivered, before we pray for them to be healed, we first need to tell them about the healing power of Jesus Christ. The reason we do that, is so that we can stir up their faith to receive the Lord's healing power, when we lay hands on them. Let me say that the only thing that can hinder an unsaved person from receiving healing from the Lord, is unbelief. Sin is not a hindrance, simply because all unbelievers are sinners. Our Lord Jesus laid His hands on all seeking to be healed through His ministry, and He has not changed one bit since then.

The early church laid hands on the unsaved

Acts 4:23-33 "And being let go, they went to their own companions and reported all that the chief priests and elders had said to them. (24) So when they heard that, they raised their voice to God with one accord and said: "Lord, You are God, who made heaven and earth and the sea, and all that is in them, ... (29) Now, Lord, look on their threats, and grant to Your servants that with all boldness they may speak Your word, (30) by stretching out Your hand to heal, and that signs and wonders may be done through the name of Your holy Servant Jesus." (31) And when they had prayed, the place where they were assembled together was shaken; and they were all filled with the Holy Spirit, and they spoke the word of God with boldness. ... (33) And with great power the apostles gave witness to the resurrection of the Lord Jesus. And great grace was upon them all."

Acts 5:12-16 "And through the hands of the apostles many signs and wonders were done among the people. And they were all with one accord in Solomon's Porch. (13) Yet none of the rest dared join them, but the people esteemed them highly. (14) And believers were increasingly added to the Lord, multitudes of both men and women, (15) so that they brought the sick out into the streets and laid them on beds and couches, that at least the shadow of Peter passing by might fall on some of them. (16) Also a multitude gathered from the surrounding cities to Jerusalem, bringing sick people and those who were tormented by unclean spirits, and they were all healed."

The saints in the book of Acts, understood that this ministry of laying on of hands on the unsaved, was for every saint land not just for a chosen few. In the above passages of scripture, we see great healing power being demonstrated through all the saints in the church at

Jerusalem. The background to this scripture is that the apostles Peter and John, had been threatened by the Jewish leaders to no longer preach in the name of Jesus. Those two apostles had called the church together to report these threats, and the church then reacted, by praying. When you read this account at first glance, it seems as if God only answered their prayers through the apostles. And it also seems as if God answered their prayers, primarily through Peter's ministry. But that is not the case at all. The reason the Holy Spirit mentions Peter and the other apostles, is because they indeed had a greater anointing to heal the sick. Because that anointing formed part of their ministry gift. And so, the greater anointing manifested through Peter, to the point that even his shadow could heal the sick. But even though the rest of the saints did not have that degree of anointing on them, they were all used by the Holy Spirit to heal the sick, through the laying on of their hands. For the scripture teaches us that all the saints prayed together in one accord, "*they raised their voice to God _with one accord_*". And all the saints were filled with the Holy Spirit because of God answering their prayers, "*and _they were all filled with the Holy Spirit_*". And again, all the saints began to speak the word of God with boldness as they witnessed to the unsaved throughout the city of Jerusalem, "*and they _... all ... spoke_ the word of God with boldness*". And again, all the saints began to minister the power of God through healing, signs and wonders. For the Lord, had given great grace to all His saints, "*and great grace _was upon them all_*". We need to understand that in the book of Acts, the Holy Spirit only highlights certain people and certain events. He does that from a practicality point of view, because it is not possible for any writer to record all that God did through His church at that time. And so, when the Holy Spirit does highlight certain key events and people, He does so, to give us examples of what is available to all His saints.

Acts 15:12 "Then all the multitude kept silent and listened to Barnabas and Paul declaring how many miracles and wonders God had worked through them among the Gentiles."

Acts 6:1-7 "Now in those days, when the number of the disciples was multiplying, there arose a complaint against the Hebrews by the Hellenists, because their widows were neglected in the daily distribution. (2) Then the twelve summoned the multitude of the disciples and said, "It is not desirable that we should leave the word of God and serve tables. (3) Therefore, brethren, seek out from among you seven men of reputation, full of the Holy Spirit and wisdom, whom we may appoint over this business; (4) but we will give ourselves continually to prayer and to the ministry of the word." (5) And the saying pleased the whole multitude. And they chose Stephen, a man full of faith and the Holy Spirit, and Philip, Prochorus, Nicanor, Timon, Parmenas, and Nicolas, a proselyte from Antioch, (6) whom they set before the apostles; and when they had prayed, they laid hands on them. (7) Then the word of God spread, and the number of the disciples multiplied greatly in Jerusalem, and a great many of the priests were obedient to the faith."

In the bible, there are not many accounts recorded, of the miracles and healings done through the apostle's ministries. But we know from scripture, that there were many that took place all the time. In the above passage of scripture quoted from Acts chapter fifteen, we see Barnabas and Paul recounting to the church at Jerusalem, just how many miracles and wonders the Lord had done through just one of their missionary journeys. And yet scripture only records two of those miracles that took place during that first missionary journey, i.e. the false prophet Elymas who was blinded, and the crippled man who was healed in Lystra. It is in that light that we need to examine just what took place among the saints, when the church first began. It was in the first few months of the church's existence that the apostles called for seven disciples to be chosen from among the church, to help with the daily distribution that was taking place. The growth in the church had exploded, and the apostles were not able to cope with everything that was happening. The scriptures tell us that these seven men were full of the Holy Spirit, and had a reputation among the saints. The reason that these men had a reputation among the saints, is because they were all being mightily used by the Holy Spirit, in the demonstration of His power. We know this, because later we see recorded in scripture, accounts of how just two of these men were used by the Lord, to heal the sick and do many wonders in His name. All these men were already being used by the Holy Spirit to perform signs and wonders, when the apostles prayed for them. In this instance, hands were laid on them for service as deacons, which we will discuss in another chapter. Clearly, in the early church the Holy Spirit used every saint that was prepared to step out in faith, and fulfill the Lord's great commission of preaching the gospel to every creature, to cast out demons and to lay hands on the sick so that they may be healed. So, let us look at the examples given to us in scripture of these ordinary saints, who cast

Laying hands on the unsaved

out demons and laid their hands on those in need of healing.

Acts 6:8 "And Stephen, full of faith and power, did great wonders and signs among the people."

Acts 8:4-7 "Therefore those who were scattered went everywhere preaching the word. (5) Then Philip went down to the city of Samaria and preached Christ to them. (6) And the multitudes with one accord heeded the things spoken by Philip, hearing and seeing the miracles which he did. (7) For unclean spirits, crying with a loud voice, came out of many who were possessed; and many who were paralyzed and lame were healed."

In the scripture quoted from Acts chapter six, the Holy Spirit tells us that Stephen did great wonders and signs among the people. If you look at the other accounts of the signs done by the apostles, you will know that the signs and wonders done through Stephen would have been signs of healings and the casting out of demons. The point that I want to make here, is that Stephen was just an ordinary saint who served at the tables, and yet he cast out demons and he laid hands on the sick and the sick were healed. In the second account quoted from Acts chapter eight, we see Philip not only preaching the gospel, but also laying his hands on the sick and casting out demons. Although the account is of what Philip did in the city of Samaria, he had already learnt to operate in the power of the Holy Spirit, while he was still a disciple in Jerusalem. Philip would have performed the exact same signs when he was in Jerusalem, just as his brother Stephen had. Someone said, but I though Philip was an evangelist. When Philip went down to Samaria, he was still just an ordinary saint who waited on the tables. It was only much later, that the Holy Spirit promoted him into the ministry of the evangelist. These are accounts in scripture, of just two of the Lord's ordinary saints healing the sick and casting out demons. As we have seen with regards to the numerous miracles performed through Paul and Barnabas, which scripture has not recorded, there were myriads of other signs performed through the ordinary saints in the early church, which have also not been recorded in scripture. But those that have been recorded, are given to us so that we can follow their example. And so, we see that all believers are well able to lay their hands on the unsaved in these two areas and expect results. Namely, laying hands on the sick so that they may recover and casting out demons.

Signs that they may be saved

Acts 9:32-35 "Now it came to pass, as Peter went through all parts of the country, that he also came down to the saints who dwelt in Lydda. (33) There he found a certain man named Aeneas, who had been bedridden eight years and was paralyzed. (34) And Peter said to him, "Aeneas, Jesus the Christ heals you. Arise and make your bed." Then he arose immediately. (35) So all who dwelt at Lydda and Sharon saw him and turned to the Lord."

Acts 14:6-22 "they became aware of it and fled to Lystra and Derbe, cities of Lycaonia, and to the surrounding region. (7) And they were preaching the gospel there. (8) And in Lystra a certain man without strength in his feet was sitting, a cripple

*from his mother's womb, who had never walked. (9)
This man heard Paul speaking. Paul, observing him
intently and seeing that he had faith to be healed,
(10) said with a loud voice, "Stand up straight on
your feet!" And he leaped and walked. (11) Now
when the people saw what Paul had done, they
raised their voices, saying in the Lycaonian
language, "The gods have come down to us in the
likeness of men!" ... (21) And when they had
preached the gospel to that city and made many
disciples, they returned to Lystra, Iconium, and
Antioch, (22) strengthening the souls of the disciples,
exhorting them to continue in the faith, and saying,
"We must through many tribulations enter the
kingdom of God."*

*1 Corinthians 14:24-25 "But if all prophesy,
and an unbeliever or an uninformed person comes
in, he is convinced by all, he is convicted by all. (25)
And thus the secrets of his heart are revealed; and
so, falling down on his face, he will worship God and
report that God is truly among you."*

So why does our Lord want His saints to lay hands
on the unsaved so that they may be healed and delivered?
You will recall that our Lord taught us that these would be
signs, that He would perform through His saints. Our
Lord Jesus performs these signs so that the unsaved may
believe in the message of the gospel, and so be saved. In
the above account quoted from Acts chapter nine, the
apostle Peter came to the town of Lydda to hold meetings
for the saints there. Peter's reputation for healing the sick
would have been widely spread throughout that area, and
many who were wanting to be healed attended his

meetings, including the unsaved. It was during this time that Peter healed Aeneas. Scripture refers to Aeneas as, "a certain man". Whenever this term is used in the book of Acts, it usually refers to one who is unsaved. And in referring to those who were saved, the term "a certain disciple" would normally be used. The Lord used Peter to heal Aeneas. And because of that sign being performed, the Holy Spirit tells us that every unsaved person in the towns of Lydda and Sharon, turned to the Lord. In the next account quoted from Acts chapter fourteen, the apostle Paul and his ministry team had come to the town of Lystra, and they were preaching the gospel there for the first time. During one of his meetings, the Lord used the apostle Paul to heal an unsaved, crippled man. Because of that sign being performed, many in Lystra and the surrounding towns, were saved. Although in this instance, because of the idol worship taking place in those cities at the time, there was the unfortunate spinoff of some of the people trying to worship Paul and Barnabas as gods, which Paul and Barnabas had to correct. And so, scripture clearly reveals to us that our Lord Jesus wants His saints to lay hands on the unsaved, so that He can perform His signs through the laying on of their hands. Our Lord performs these signs so that the unsaved may believe the message of the gospel, and thus be saved. Although the gift of the word of knowledge is not always used through the laying on of hands, the Holy Spirit does also make this gift manifest to minister to the unsaved. He does this, so that the unsaved can recognize the power of God and believe in Him, and thus be saved. Clearly from the scripture quoted from Corinthians, we can see that it is the will of the Holy Spirit that we as believers, allow Him to make Himself manifest through us in this gift of the word of knowledge, specifically in ministering to the unsaved. The whole purpose of this gift being used for the unsaved is so that they can recognize that God is real, and that He is in the church. The result of them encountering the supernatural power of God will be that they will give their lives to the Lord. As believers, we should expect the Holy Spirit to use us in this manner in ministering the supernatural power of God to the unsaved, and yield to Him when He does.

We are to be walking epistles

Matthew 8:16-17 "When evening had come, they brought to Him many who were demon-possessed. And He cast out the spirits with a word, and healed all who were sick, (17) that it might be fulfilled which was spoken by Isaiah the prophet, saying: "HE HIMSELF TOOK OUR INFIRMITIES AND BORE OUR SICKNESSES."

Galatians 3:13 "Christ has redeemed us from the curse of the law, having become a curse for us (for it is written, "CURSED IS EVERYONE WHO HANGS ON A TREE").

1 Peter 2:24 "who Himself bore our sins in His own body on the tree, that we, having died to sins, might live for righteousness--by whose stripes you were healed."

Our Lord Jesus not only bore all our sins, but God's word teaches us that when He went to the cross, He also took all our sickness and disease. The bible tells us that out of the mouth of two or three witnesses, let every word be established. I have quoted three different writers from the new testament, who all say the same thing. All three tell us that when Jesus took our sins on the cross, He also took our sickness. Matthew tells us that our Lord Jesus took our infirmities and bore our diseases. All Christians have no problem believing that Jesus took their sins, but struggle to believe that Jesus also took their sickness. And yet that is exactly what God's word says. Peter tells us that by the stripes of our Lord Jesus, that we were healed. The term "were healed", is past tense. That means that all of God's children have a right to be healed in the present tense. Again, all Christians have no problem believing the first part of that verse, in that Jesus bore their sins on the tree. But many struggle to believe the second part of the same verse of scripture, i.e. by His stripes we were healed. And the apostle Paul tell us, that our Lord Jesus has redeemed us from the curse of the law. If you read the curse of the law in Deuteronomy chapter twenty-eight, you will see that every sickness and every disease, is included under the curse of the law. And so, what Paul is telling the body of Christ, is that Christ has redeemed us from all sickness and all disease. As far as God is concerned it has all been done, and whether we believe it or not does not change the fact that Jesus has done it. Salvation works in the same manner. Our Lord Jesus has died for everyone, and He has born everyone's sin. Whether we believe that or not, does not change the fact that Jesus has done it. Those who choose not to believe that Jesus has born their sins, do not experience salvation through the new birth. But those who do choose to believe that Jesus has born their sins, experience salvation through the new birth. In the same manner those who choose not to believe that Jesus has born their sickness, do not receive divine health for the physical bodies. But those who do choose to believe that Jesus has born their sickness, will experience divine health in their physical bodies. Unless you believe that healing and divine health belongs to those who have been redeemed, and are walking in the light of that truth, you will not be very effective in fulfilling the Lord's mandate to lay hands on the unsaved for their healing. When I say that you need to be walking in that truth, I mean that you should be walking in the divine health delivered to us by the stripes of our Lord Jesus. We have seen in this chapter that our Lord Jesus has called each one of His saints to lay hands on the unsaved. We are to lay hands on the unsaved who are sick, so that they may recover. And we are to lay hands on the unsaved, to cast out the demons that are holding them in bondage. It is mainly in the areas of healing and deliverance, that we lay hands on the unsaved. You will recall that I emphasized in the previous chapter, that faith is required for the laying on of hands to work. For the child of God to be effective in laying hands on the unsaved, you are going to have to have an unwavering faith in the healing power of our Lord Jesus. And you are also going to have to have an unwavering faith in the fact that it is our Lord's will to heal all today, including the unsaved. Jesus Christ is the same yesterday, today and forever. Our Lord has never, and will never, change. In that light, look at the following scriptures.

Acts 10:38 "how God anointed Jesus of Nazareth with the Holy Spirit and with power, who went about doing good and healing all who were oppressed by the devil, for God was with Him."

1 John 3:8 "For this purpose the Son of God was manifested, that He might destroy the works of the devil."

Laying hands on the unsaved

Mark 3:27 "No one can enter a strong man's house and plunder his goods, unless he first binds the strong man. And then he will plunder his house."

When our Lord Jesus walked in the flesh, He destroyed the works of the devil. Our Lord Jesus did that by healing the sick, casting out demons, raising the dead and preaching the gospel to the poor. In the book of Acts, the bible reveals to us that Jesus went about doing good and healing all. That same scripture reveals to us that the ones that our Lord Jesus healed, were those who were oppressed by the devil. Clearly sickness is from the devil, and healing is from the Lord. The Lord Jesus Christ, who dwells within each one of His saints, still has the same mandate from God the Father. It is still the Lord's express will and mandate, to destroy the works of the devil. And He still does that, by healing all who are oppressed by the devil. But He can only do that work through His church, which represents Him in the earth today. For we are His body. There is no record in scripture of a blind person laying hands on another blind person, in order to get them healed. What do I mean by that statement? Remember that we said that for the laying on of hands to be able to work, faith is required to be operating in both parties. If you are going to witness to the unsaved about the healing power of Jesus, then for their faith to be activated, the unsaved are going to have to see evidence of His healing power in you. You are going to have a hard time trying to convince an unsaved person that God can heal them, if they can clearly see that you yourself are sick. Again, it becomes difficult, though not impossible, for one to have faith for others to be healed if you cannot exercise faith for your own healing and health. In the above passage of scripture quoted from Mark's gospel, our Lord Jesus is clearly teaching us how to go about destroying the works of our adversary, the devil. We go into his territory to destroy his works. For the world is his territory, as scripture plainly tells us that he is the god of this world. And as the god of this world, all unbelievers are to a greater or lesser degree, under his control. Those among them who are sick, are sick because Satan has put sickness on them. Our Lord has taught us that if we are to be able to plunder the house of our adversary, then we are going to have to first bind him. And it becomes impossible to bind the devil in this area, if he himself has the saint bound in sickness.

Chapter 3
Laying hands on believers

To be filled with the Holy Spirit

Luke 3:16 "John answered, saying to all, "I indeed baptize you with water; but One mightier than I is coming, whose sandal strap I am not worthy to loose. He will baptize you with the Holy Spirit and fire."

Acts 10:44-47 "While Peter was still speaking these words, the Holy Spirit fell upon all those who heard the word. (45) And those of the circumcision who believed were astonished, as many as came with Peter, because the gift of the Holy Spirit had been poured out on the Gentiles also. (46) For they heard them speak with tongues and magnify God. Then Peter answered, (47) "Can anyone forbid water, that these should not be baptized who have received the Holy Spirit just as we have?"

Acts 19:1-7 "And it happened, while Apollos was at Corinth, that Paul, having passed through the upper regions, came to Ephesus. And finding some disciples (2) he said to them, "Did you receive the Holy Spirit when you believed?" So they said to him, "We have not so much as heard whether there is a Holy Spirit." (3) And he said to them, "Into what then were you baptized?" So they said, "Into John's baptism." (4) Then Paul said, "John indeed baptized with a baptism of repentance, saying to the people

Laying hands on believers

that they should believe on Him who would come after him, that is, on Christ Jesus." (5) When they heard this, they were baptized in the name of the Lord Jesus. (6) And when Paul had laid hands on them, the Holy Spirit came upon them, and they spoke with tongues and prophesied. (7) Now the men were about twelve in all."

In scripture, we see two methods that our Lord uses to fill His saints with the Holy Spirit. The first is directly from Him, for He is the one who baptizes with the Holy Spirit, anyway. I refer to this method, as being filled directly from heaven. In the above passage of scripture quoted from Luke's gospel, John the Baptist taught us that it is Jesus Himself who baptizes us with the Holy Spirit. And we saw evidence of that taking place in the earlier account that we looked at, when the disciples were filled with the Holy Spirit on the day of Pentecost. For the scripture tells us that the sound of the mighty rushing wind came from heaven. Acts chapter ten quoted above, is another account in scripture, where the saints were filled with the Holy Spirit directly from heaven, without anyone laying hands on them. This is the account, when through Peter the apostle, the gentiles heard the gospel preached for the first time. In my own experience, I was filled with the Holy Spirit in this manner. I had been born again for less than a week, when some fellow Christians invited me to attend a bible conference. I had never been to such an event before, and when I got there I was introduced to other believers, as a brand-new convert. One of the believers I was introduced to, asked me if I had received the Holy Spirit and spoken in tongues since I was saved. I had no idea what the person was talking about, and the people who brought me to the meeting told me not to worry about it, because they would explain that all to me at a later stage. The meeting then began, as the saints began to worship the Lord. Halfway through the worship, the power of God came all over me and I just knew that if I spoke out, I would speak in those tongues that I had just heard about. And so, I spoke out, and have been speaking in tongues ever since. Altogether, there are six accounts given as examples in the book of Acts and the epistles, of the saints being filled with the Holy Spirit. Of the six, two are accounts where the saints were filled directly from heaven, and four were accounts of the saints being filled with the Holy Spirit through the laying on of hands. Of the accounts where the Lord filled the saints directly from heaven, the first was on the day of Pentecost which we have already looked at. Then there was also the account that we have just read, of the gentiles being filled with the Holy Spirit directly from heaven. We then we come to the second method, that our Lord uses to fill His saints with the Holy Spirit. And that method is through the laying on of hands. Of the four accounts where the laying on of hands was used to fill the saints with the Holy Spirit, we have already looked at the account earlier, of when Peter and John went to Samaria to lay hands on the new converts, for them to receive the Holy Spirit. In the above account in scripture, Paul the apostle, laid hands on these new believers in Ephesus, and they were then filled with the Holy Spirit and spoke with tongues. In this instance, they also received one of the gifts of the Holy Spirit at the same time, for scripture reveals to us that they prophesied.

Acts 9:17 "And Ananias went his way and entered the house; and laying his hands on him he said, "Brother Saul, the Lord Jesus, who appeared to you on the road as you came, has sent me that you may receive your sight and be filled with the Holy Spirit."

2 Timothy 1:6-7 "Therefore I remind you to stir up the gift of God which is in you through the laying on of my hands. (7) For God has not given us a spirit of fear, but of power and of love and of a sound mind."

In the account quoted from Acts chapter nine, the disciple Ananias was sent by the Lord Jesus to lay his hands on Paul, so that he could receive his sight and be filled with the Holy Spirit. We know that when Paul was filled with the Holy Spirit that he spoke with tongues, because he said to the church at Corinth that he thanked God that he spoke with tongues more than all. In the passage of scripture from Second Timothy, Paul reminds Timothy that he received the baptism of the Holy Spirit through the laying on of Paul's hands. And Paul encourages Timothy to stir up the gift of the Holy Spirit that is within him. Because Paul tells him that he had not received a spirit of fear, but rather a Spirit of power, love and a sound mind. The fact that there are four accounts in scripture, of being filled with the Holy Spirit through the laying on of hands, and half that number of accounts of being filled directly from heaven, indicates to us that the laying on of hands is the most common method used by the Lord to fill His saints. Both methods require faith on the part of the recipient, in order to be able to be filled. This fact points us to the reason as to why the Lord uses the laying on of hands method more frequently, to fill His saints. Because the laying on of hands is a method that assists the recipient to be able to release their faith when the point of contact is made through the laying on of hands. But we must also not forget that, as we discussed earlier, there are certain individuals who receive this specific anointing from the Lord to lay hands on believers for the infilling of the Holy Spirit. Because these individuals are anointed in this area, they will always have more success when they lay hands on individuals to be filled with the Spirit.

Speaking and revelation gifts

Genesis 48:10-20 "Now the eyes of Israel were dim with age, so that he could not see. Then Joseph brought them near him, and he kissed them and embraced them. (11) And Israel said to Joseph, "I had not thought to see your face; but in fact, God has also shown me your offspring!" (12) So Joseph brought them from beside his knees, and he bowed down with his face to the earth. (13) And Joseph took them both, Ephraim with his right hand toward Israel's left hand, and Manasseh with his left hand toward Israel's right hand, and brought them near him. (14) Then Israel stretched out his right hand and laid it on Ephraim's head, who was the younger, and his left hand on Manasseh's head, guiding his hands knowingly, for Manasseh was the firstborn. (15) And he blessed Joseph, and said: "God, before whom my fathers Abraham and Isaac walked, The God who has fed me all my life long to this day, (16) The Angel who has redeemed me from all evil, Bless the lads; Let my name be named upon them, And the name of my fathers Abraham and Isaac; And let them grow into a multitude in the midst of the earth." (17) Now when Joseph saw that his father laid his right hand on the head of Ephraim, it displeased him; so he took hold of his father's hand to remove it from Ephraim's head to Manasseh's head. (18) And Joseph said to his father, "Not so, my father, for this one is the firstborn; put your right hand on his head." (19) But his father refused and said, "I know, my son, I know. He also shall become a people, and he also shall be great; but truly his younger brother shall be greater than he, and his descendants shall become a multitude of nations." (20) So he blessed them that day, saying, "By you Israel will bless, saying, 'May God make you as Ephraim and as Manasseh!' " And thus he set Ephraim before Manasseh."

1 Timothy 4:14 "Do not neglect the gift that is in you, which was given to you by prophecy with the laying on of the hands of the eldership."

In this section, we will see that both the speaking and the revelation gifts of the Spirit can and should, also be manifested through the laying on of hands. Under the Old Covenant, the same gifts of the Spirit were manifested as are manifested under the New Covenant, except for tongues and the interpretation of tongues. In the first example that we will look at, we can see both the gift of prophecy and the gift of the word of knowledge being made manifest through the laying on of hands. In the above passage of scripture as quoted from the book of Genesis, we have an account of Israel prophesying over two of his grandsons, Ephraim and Manasseh. Israel prophesied over them through the laying on of hands. The gift of the word of knowledge was also manifested through his prophecy, because he prophesied that Ephraim would be greater than Manasseh, as God had intended. It is interesting to note in this account, that with regards to the blessing aspect of the laying on of hands, that God places more emphasis on placing the right hand on the person. But with regards to prophetic words spoken over an individual, this is not the case. For Israel prophesied over both boys accurately, through the laying on of both his right and left hands. In the account quoted from first Timothy, we have another example given to us in the New Testament, of the speaking and revelation gifts being made manifest through the laying on of hands. In this passage of scripture, Paul reminded Timothy that the elders had laid hands on Timothy, and at the same time they had spoken prophetic words over his life. Again, in this example there were two gifts of the Spirit manifested through the laying on of hands. The first was the gift of prophecy, for Paul said that prophecy was used. The second gift that was manifested was the gift of the word of knowledge. For the prophetic word given to Timothy told him what spiritual gift the Holy Spirit had imparted to him. Obviously, that was an accurate word given, because Paul had then witnessed Timothy begin to operate in that gift. And so, in his letter to Timothy, the apostle Paul encourages Timothy not to neglect that gift, but to continue to use it for the edification of the church.

Acts 9:17 "And Ananias went his way and entered the house; and laying his hands on him he said, "Brother Saul, the Lord Jesus, who appeared to you on the road as you came, has sent me that you may receive your sight and be filled with the Holy Spirit."

Laying hands on believers

Acts 22:12-16 "Then a certain Ananias, a devout man according to the law, having a good testimony with all the Jews who dwelt there, (13) came to me; and he stood and said to me, 'Brother Saul, receive your sight.' And at that same hour I looked up at him. (14) Then he said, 'The God of our fathers has chosen you that you should know His will, and see the Just One, and hear the voice of His mouth. (15) For you will be His witness to all men of what you have seen and heard. (16) And now why are you waiting? Arise and be baptized, and wash away your sins, calling on the name of the Lord."

In this next account in scripture, we see in chapter nine of the book of Acts, Ananias laying hands on the apostle Paul. Later in chapter twenty-two, when Paul recounts this event, he elaborates on what Ananias spoke over Paul when he laid his hands on him. Ananias gave Paul a word of knowledge, in that he told Paul that God had chosen him to know the will of God and to be His witness to all men. And so, we can see clearly in scripture, that the speaking and revelation gifts can also operate through the laying on of hands. Not only can these gifts operate through the laying on of hands, but they should be encouraged to operate through this method. The church has neglected this aspect of ministry, and thus missed out on the blessing that the Lord intended for His church. In my ministry, the Lord has used me to give words of wisdom and words of knowledge prophetically, both through just speaking to individuals and also through the laying on of hands. However, I have always found that the most accurate words that I bring, are through the laying on of hands. In fact, sometimes I know that the Lord wants me to give a word to an individual but I must lay hands on that individual, before that word is released through me.

Healing and raising the dead

Philippians 2:25-30 "Yet I considered it necessary to send to you Epaphroditus, my brother, fellow worker, and fellow soldier, but your messenger and the one who ministered to my need; (26) since he was longing for you all, and was distressed because you had heard that he was sick. (27) For indeed he was sick almost unto death; but God had mercy on him, and not only on him but on me also, lest I should have sorrow upon sorrow. (28) Therefore I sent him the more eagerly, that when you see him again you may rejoice, and I may be less sorrowful. (29) Receive him therefore in the Lord with all gladness, and hold such men in esteem; (30) because for the work of Christ he came close to death, not regarding his life, to supply what was lacking in your service toward me."

2 Timothy 4:20 "Erastus stayed in Corinth, but Trophimus I have left in Miletus sick."

1 Timothy 5:23 "No longer drink only water, but use a little wine for your stomach's sake and your frequent infirmities."

As we saw earlier in this teaching, the Lord's best is for His children to walk in divine health. However, baby Christians that have not yet been taught God's word regarding the healing that He has provided for us, are in that light like the unsaved, in that they don't know any better. And so, for several reasons, when baby Christians get sick, it is that much easier to lay hands on them to be healed. As with the unsaved, the only hindrance to baby Christians receiving healing from the Lord, is unbelief. And normally unbelief is not a problem, because as newly saved, they are more receptive to God's healing power. I recall on one occasion that I prayed for a woman who had recently been saved, and who was deaf in one ear. I told her about the healing power of the Lord Jesus and that it was a very small thing for Him who created her ear, to restore hearing to that ear. I personally like to use the word "expect" when I am about to lay hands on individuals, because it is a word that is more easily understood in today's vernacular. And so, I said to her that when I laid hands on her that she should expect God to heal her ear, and that is exactly what He would do. I asked her if she was ready to receive her healing when I laid hands on her, and she eagerly answered that she was. You could tell by her countenance, that she was in faith. She was expecting to be healed. The moment I put my finger in her ear and prayed it felt like static electricity jumped from my finger into her ear (remember we spoke about the transference God's of power through the laying on of hands) and she was instantly healed. I have quoted several scriptures above, all of them relating to sickness in Christians. As we look at these scriptures we can learn some truths as to why it is that Christians become sick, and what they can do to be healed. The first account quoted, is of Epaphroditus. He was an apostle. The word translated "messenger" in this passage, is translated "apostle" elsewhere in scripture. He had become sick because he had neglected his physical health. Even though he was working for Christ, he had driven his body too hard by taking on too much, and it eventually affected his health. Therefore, Paul states that the Lord had mercy on Epaphroditus in healing him. The reason he needed the Lord's mercy, was because he had been disobedient in that he had not looked after his body as the Lord expects us to. God expects us to use wisdom, and take care of the bodies that He has given us. As we do our part in the natural by taking care of our bodies, He then does His part in the supernatural, by keeping us from sickness. The second account quoted is of Trophimus. Trophimus had been a part of Pauls' ministry team for several years and had travelled with him extensively. He joined Paul's ministry team in Ephesus and travelled with him to Jerusalem and many other cities. But in Pauls' letter to Timothy, all Paul states is that he had left Trophimus sick in the town of Miletus. Scripture gives us no insight into why Trophimus became sick. But it does tell us plainly that the apostle Paul was not able to lay hands on him to be healed. We saw earlier where Paul laid hands on the sick in Malta, and they were all healed. If it were up to Paul, he would have laid his hands on Trophimus to be healed just like he did at the island of Malta. The difference between Trophimus and the people of Malta however, was that the people of Malta were unsaved, whereas Trophimus was a believer who had been saved for many years. Trophimus' healing was between himself and the Lord. The third account quoted is of Timothy. In his letter to Timothy, Paul instructs Timothy to start using a little wine instead of just water, because he was suffering from frequent infirmities. Again, scripture does not reveal to us just why Timothy was suffering these infirmities. But as with Trophimus, we know that Timothy had also been part of Paul's ministry team for many years. Again, if Paul could just lay hands on Timothy to heal him, he would have done so. But clearly this was not possible. And so, Timothy's healing was also between himself and the Lord.

1 Corinthians 11:30-32 "For this reason many are weak and sick among you, and many sleep. (31) For if we would judge ourselves, we would not be judged. (32) But when we are judged, we are chastened by the Lord, that we may not be condemned with the world."

James 5:14-16 "Is anyone among you sick? Let him call for the elders of the church, and let them pray over him, anointing him with oil in the name of the Lord. (15) And the prayer of faith will save the sick, and the Lord will raise him up. And if he has committed sins, he will be forgiven. (16) Confess your trespasses to one another, and pray for one another, that you may be healed. The effective, fervent prayer of a righteous man avails much."

Revelation 2:21-22 "And I gave her time to repent of her sexual immorality, and she did not repent. (22) Indeed I will cast her into a sickbed, and those who commit adultery with her into great tribulation, unless they repent of their deeds."

We have had a look at scriptural accounts of believers who had been saved for many years, and became sick. There are four main reasons why Christians can become sick. The first reason is because of ignorance i.e. they do not know what God's word says about healing for believers, under the new covenant. This group of believers treat sickness as a natural part of life, and deal with it as such, i.e. through medical treatments that are available to them. The second reason is because they know what God's word says, but they don't believe it, i.e. they are not fully convinced in their minds that healing is provided for them, and so their faith is weak in this area. This group of believers therefore also deal with sickness through medical treatments that are available to them. The third reason is because they do not look after their physical bodies, as we have seen in the case of Epaphroditus. God is not mocked. We cannot neglect our bodies through substance abuse, gluttony, lack of proper exercise and then expect Him to keep our bodies healthy. And then we come to the fourth reason. I have quoted three scriptures above from the new testament, that all deal with sickness among Christians. All three of them link sickness in believers, to sin. Clearly in these scriptures, our Lord Jesus uses sickness as a form of chastening for those of His children, who are walking in unrepentant sin. And so, when it comes to laying hands on believers for healing, who have been saved for several years, there are two hindrances that must first be dealt with. Firstly, their faith level must be increased through hearing God's word regarding healing, and that normally takes a little time. Then secondly, any unrepentant sin must be dealt with, through repentance and forgiveness. Once those conditions are met, then there will be no hindrance to that believer receiving their healing from the Lord, through the laying on of hands.

Acts 9:36-42 "At Joppa there was a certain disciple named Tabitha, which is translated Dorcas. This woman was full of good works and charitable deeds which she did. (37) But it happened in those days that she became sick and died. When they had washed her, they laid her in an upper room. (38)

Laying hands on believers

And since Lydda was near Joppa, and the disciples had heard that Peter was there, they sent two men to him, imploring him not to delay in coming to them. (39) Then Peter arose and went with them. When he had come, they brought him to the upper room. And all the widows stood by him weeping, showing the tunics and garments which Dorcas had made while she was with them. (40) But Peter put them all out, and knelt down and prayed. And turning to the body he said, "Tabitha, arise." And she opened her eyes, and when she saw Peter she sat up. (41) Then he gave her his hand and lifted her up; and when he had called the saints and widows, he presented her alive. (42) And it became known throughout all Joppa, and many believed on the Lord."

Acts 20:8-12 "There were many lamps in the upper room where they were gathered together. (9) And in a window sat a certain young man named Eutychus, who was sinking into a deep sleep. He was overcome by sleep; and as Paul continued speaking, he fell down from the third story and was taken up dead. (10) But Paul went down, fell on him, and embracing him said, "Do not trouble yourselves, for his life is in him." (11) Now when he had come up, had broken bread and eaten, and talked a long while, even till daybreak, he departed. (12) And they brought the young man in alive, and they were not a little comforted."

We saw with regards to the accounts of healing in the book of Acts, that it was significant that every account mentioned, related to believers ministering to the unsaved. The reason for that is because the ministry of laying on of hands as far as healing is concerned, is mainly for the unsaved. But when it comes to laying on of hands to raise the dead, then this ministry is only for the saved. In both accounts given to us in the book of Acts, the people who were raised from the dead, were believers. The reason for that is simple. When believers die, their spirits go to heaven. Because they go to heaven they can return to the earth to reenter their bodies, if they are instructed to, by the Lord. In the above instances, both Peter and Paul would have called for the spirits of these deceased disciples, to be returned to the earth. Because both Peter and Paul prayed in faith, and it was only their faith that was involved, our Lord honored their faith, and instructed the two disciples in question, to return to the earth. In the incident where Peter was involved, he had to put everyone out of the room before he prayed. He did so because raising the dead requires faith, with no presence of doubt. Peter learnt this lesson, when he watched Jesus raise the little girl from the dead. The incident where Paul was involved, was a little different. In Paul's case, no one expected Paul to do what he did. Paul just went down, fell on the young man and raised him from the dead, and so no one had any time to doubt. Jesus did the same thing when He raised the young man in Nain. No one suspected that Jesus was going to raise him from the dead. And so even though there were many people present, there was no unbelief manifested to hinder that miracle from happening. The two disciples mentioned above, would have had to be sent back by the Lord, because of their own volition they would not have wanted to return. No believer, once they have entered heaven to be with the Lord, ever wants to return to the earth. For it is far better to depart and to be with Christ. Besides believers, children can also be raised from the dead. It is not possible to raise unbelievers from the dead however, because their spirits go to hell. And no one that goes to hell can ever come out of there. They will only be released from hades on the day of judgement to face their eternal judgement.

Imparting gifts of the Spirit

Numbers 27:18-23 "And the LORD said to Moses: "Take Joshua the son of Nun with you, a man in whom is the Spirit, and lay your hand on him; (19) set him before Eleazar the priest and before all the congregation, and inaugurate him in their sight. (20) And you shall give some of your authority to him, that all the congregation of the children of Israel may be obedient. ... (22) So Moses did as the LORD commanded him. He took Joshua and set him before Eleazar the priest and before all the congregation. (23) And he laid his hands on him and inaugurated him, just as the LORD commanded by the hand of Moses."

Deuteronomy 34:9 "Now Joshua the son of Nun was full of the spirit of wisdom, for Moses had laid his hands on him; so, the children of Israel heeded him, and did as the LORD had commanded Moses."

There are two aspects to the laying on of hands, that we see in these portions of scripture. The one is inauguration, and the other is the transference of anointing. In this section of the teaching we want to look at the aspect of transference of the anointing. The context of these scriptures is that Moses was about to leave the children of Israel, as his time to die had come. God had raised up Joshua in his place, to carry on leading the children of Israel into their promised land. God then instructed Moses to lay hands on Joshua to invest him with this new office, in which he now had to stand i.e. to be the new leader of Israel. You will notice that even before Moses laid hands on Joshua that Joshua already had the Holy Spirit on him, *"a man in whom is the Spirit"*. In other words, God had already called Joshua and recognized him, by giving him the Holy Spirit. Now that Joshua was about to take on a new role, he needed the appropriate anointing to do that. God said to Moses that he was to give Joshua authority, *"And you shall give some of your authority to him"*. In this instance, there was a definite transference of anointing from Moses to Joshua. We see that, because in the passage in Deuteronomy, the Holy Spirit reveals to us that Joshua was full of the spirit of wisdom, specifically because Moses had laid hands on him. Moses had that anointing on his ministry, and now he was being used by God to impart that same anointing to Joshua. This account in the Old Testament, of the laying on of hands for the impartation of God's power, gives us some insight regarding how this ministry operates in the New Testament. One of those insights is that the one who is being used to impart the anointing, must have that anointing themselves. Because as we have read, Moses gave Joshua of the authority and wisdom that he himself had.

Acts 19:6 "And when Paul had laid hands on them, the Holy Spirit came upon them, and they spoke with tongues and prophesied."

1 Corinthians 12:8-11 "for to one is given the word of wisdom through the Spirit, to another the word of knowledge through the same Spirit, (9) to another faith by the same Spirit, to another gifts of healings by the same Spirit, (10) to another the working of miracles, to another prophecy, to another discerning of spirits, to another different kinds of tongues, to another the interpretation of tongues. (11) But one and the same Spirit works all these things, distributing to each one individually as He wills."

Under the new covenant there are two primary areas where impartation can take place, through the laying on of hands. The first is the infilling of the Holy Spirit, which we have already looked at earlier. Only those who have already been filled with the Holy Spirit, can lay hands on others to be filled with the Holy Spirit. The second area where impartation can take place, is in the gifts of the Spirit. The above listed gifts, are the nine gifts of the Holy Spirit. It is the Holy Spirit who imparts spiritual gifts, and not man. Sometimes the Holy Spirit will use a man to impart one of the gifts through the laying on of hands, but He is not limited to this method only. He can choose to simply drop a gift into the spirit of a believer, as He wills. So, we see that though the Holy Spirit may use a man to impart a spiritual gift, it is not the man who decides which gifts are given to whom. The man who may be used to impart a spiritual gift to another, is simply a vessel that the Holy Spirit uses at that time. These gifts are given by the Holy Spirit, as He wills. But just as the Holy Spirit cannot use one who has not been filled with the Holy Spirit, to fill someone else with the Holy Spirit. In the same manner, the Holy Spirit can only use one who has the gift of prophecy for example, to lay hands on another, to impart the gift of prophecy to that person. In the above instance recorded in the book of Acts, Paul laid hands on those disciples to receive the baptism of the Holy Spirit. When he laid his hands on them they received the baptism of the Holy Spirit, but in this instance, they also received the spiritual gift of prophecy. When Paul laid his hands on these new converts, he was expecting to fill them with the Holy Spirit. For if you read the account in scripture, you will see that that was his opening question to them. He asked them if they had received the Holy Spirit since they had believed. Paul then found out that they hadn't been saved yet, and because of Paul's witnessing to them, they were saved. And now Paul was laying his hands on them, to be filled with the Holy Spirit. But in this instance these new converts received more than just the filling of the Holy Spirit. They also received the spiritual gift of prophecy. Paul did not ask the Lord to give them this gift. The Holy Spirit gave them the gift of prophecy, as He willed. These disciples received the gift of prophecy through the laying on of hands by the apostle Paul, because he was anointed with that same gift. Different ministry gifts carry different anointing's and are also endowed with different spiritual gifts. The ministry gift of the apostle is endowed with all nine spiritual gifts, and so you can readily see that this ministry gift would therefore be able to be used by the Holy Spirit more effectively, to impart His gifts to the church.

Romans 1:11 "For I long to see you, that I may impart to you some spiritual gift, so that you may be established."

Laying hands on believers

1 Timothy 4:14 "Do not neglect the gift that is in you, which was given to you by prophecy with the laying on of the hands of the eldership."

We have already looked at the scripture in first Timothy, with regards to how prophetic words are given, through the laying on of hands. But this same scripture clearly reveals to us that spiritual gifts are also imparted, through the laying on of hands. In this account, Timothy had received a spiritual gift and that gift had been named, through the prophetic word given. Prophecy is divine utterance given by the Holy Spirit. The person prophesying in this instance, would have found out the same time that Timothy did, regarding what spiritual gift was being given by the Holy Spirit. And so, we see that man is simply the vessel used by the Holy Spirit to impart His gifts, through the laying on of hands. In the above scripture quoted from the book of Romans, we again see that it is the Holy Spirit who decides what gift is given. Paul knew that the Holy Spirit used him to impart spiritual gifts, which is why he made this comment to the church at Rome. Notice that Paul said *"that I may impart to you some spiritual gift"*. Paul did not know what spiritual gift he would impart; he only knew that the Holy Spirit would use him in that manner. As we have already seen, only those who already have a specific anointing upon them, can then be used by the Holy Spirit to impart those same spiritual gifts to others. But scripture clearly teaches us that spiritual gifts, can be imparted through the laying on of hands.

Separation and inauguration

Laying hands on believers

Numbers 8:5-18 "Then the LORD spoke to Moses, saying: ... (9) And you shall bring the Levites before the tabernacle of meeting, and you shall gather together the whole congregation of the children of Israel. (10) So you shall bring the Levites before the LORD, and the children of Israel shall lay their hands on the Levites; ... (14) Thus you shall separate the Levites from among the children of Israel, and the Levites shall be Mine. (15) After that the Levites shall go in to service the tabernacle of meeting. So you shall cleanse them and offer them like a wave offering. (16) For they are wholly given to Me from among the children of Israel; I have taken them for Myself instead of all who open the womb, the firstborn of all the children of Israel. (17) For all the firstborn among the children of Israel are Mine, both man and beast; on the day that I struck all the firstborn in the land of Egypt I sanctified them to Myself. (18) I have taken the Levites instead of all the firstborn of the children of Israel."

Acts 13:1-3 "Now in the church that was at Antioch there were certain prophets and teachers: Barnabas, Simeon who was called Niger, Lucius of Cyrene, Manaen who had been brought up with Herod the tetrarch, and Saul. (2) As they ministered to the Lord and fasted, the Holy Spirit said, "Now separate to Me Barnabas and Saul for the work to which I have called them." (3) Then, having fasted and prayed, and laid hands on them, they sent them away."

Galatians 1:15-16 "But when it pleased God, who separated me from my mother's womb and

*called me through His grace, (16) to reveal His Son
in me, that I might preach Him among the Gentiles, I
did not immediately confer with flesh and blood."*

When God instructs His people to lay hands on one
another, something always takes place in the spirit. In the
portion of scripture quoted from the book of Numbers, we
see the children of Israel being instructed by God, to lay
their hands on the Levites. Why did our Lord do this? He
told them that He had chosen the Levites to serve Him in
the tabernacle. Our Lord told the children of Israel that
He had already sanctified to Himself all their firstborn,
and they belonged to Him. And so instead of having the
firstborn of every family in Israel come and serve Him in
the tabernacle, He had now taken the whole tribe of Levi
in their place. Because the Levites were now standing
before the Lord in their place (as a replacement), the Lord
then instructed the children of Israel to lay their hands on
the Levites. In other words, the firstborn of Israel had
already been anointed by God, for service to Him. And
when the children of Israel then laid their hands on the
Levites, God caused a transference of that anointing to
take place from Israel to the Levites. From that moment,
the Levites now carried that anointing for service to God.
Notice that the Lord had already taken the Levites for
Himself i.e. they had already been separated to God for
service to Him. The Levites did not take this service on
themselves, and the children of Israel did not appoint
them to this service, God did. God then required the
children of Israel to acknowledge in the natural i.e.
through the laying on of hands, that which He had already
declared done in the spirit. When the children of Israel
laid hands on the Levites, God caused a separation to take
place in the spirit realm, and from then on, the Levites

were separated to the service of God. In the kingdom of God, there are different levels of separation unto Him. The reason for that, is because there are different offices that the Lord has put in place in His kingdom. Each office has its own purpose, as ordained by God. Only those whom God separates to an office, can stand in that office. Under the Old Covenant, the Levites were separated from the rest of the children of Israel to serve the Lord in His tabernacle. But then from among the Levites, there were the descendants of Aaron who were further separated to serve the Lord, as priests. And then from among the priests, there were those who were separated even further, to serve as High Priests before the Lord. Judgement always fell quickly, on any who presumed to stand in an office that God had not separated them to. Korah and his fellow Levites, presumed to stand in the office of priest, to which the Lord had not separated them, and God judged them with fire, as recounted to us in Numbers chapter sixteen. Under the New Covenant, God still has different levels of separation unto Himself. In this covenant, all saints are separated from the world unto God as His priests. In the ministry gifts, there are further levels of separation to the Lord.

In the above passage of scripture in Galatians, Paul reveals to us that the Lord had separated him from his mother's womb, for the ministry of preaching the gospel. That separation applies to all whom the Lord calls to full time ministry, through whichever ministry gift that He has given them. In the passage of scripture quoted above from the book of Acts, Barnabas and the other ministers in Antioch at the time (there were five in all) would also have been separated from their mother's womb, for the preaching of the gospel. Then we see the Holy Spirit telling them to further separate Paul and Barnabas to

Him, for the work that He had called them to. At the time of this incident, Paul and Barnabas were in fulltime ministry, and they had both been in the ministry for over fifteen years already. Paul at that time, stood in the offices of prophet and teacher, and Barnabas stood in the office of prophet. Because both men had proven faithful in their ministries, the Holy Spirit then moved both men into the office of apostle. Had they not proven to be faithful in their ministries, the Holy Spirit would not have moved them into the office of apostle, even though that was their ultimate calling. Notice that the Holy Spirit had already called them to this office, but now was God's time for them to be released into the office of the apostle. That office required a further separation to the Lord, because that office carried a stronger anointing and more authority in the church. Paul and Barnabas did not take the ministry of apostle on themselves, and the church did not appoint them to this ministry, God did. God then required the church to acknowledge in the natural i.e. through the laying on of hands, that which He had already declared done in the spirit. When the other ministry gifts laid hands on Paul and Barnabas, God caused a separation to take place in the spirit realm and from then on Paul and Barnabas were separated to the service of God, in the ministry of the apostle. Notice also that all the ministry gifts involved, gave themselves to further prayer and fasting before they laid hands on Paul and Barnabas. The early church took this act of laying on of hands, very seriously. Let's look at the timeline of this event, so that we can better understand what took place with the laying on of hands on this occasion. When the five ministers were fasting, and praying to the Lord, the Holy Spirit revealed His will. Barnabas and Paul didn't then leave in the middle of the night, without telling anyone. Not at all, for remember that Paul and Barnabas had been ministering in the church at Antioch for well over a year by that time. So, what happened is that they would have assembled the whole church at Antioch, to inform them what the Holy Spirit had decided. And when the whole church was present as witnesses, they laid hands on them and sent them out. Notice also, that the Holy Spirit had already called them to the office of apostle. And so, there was no impartation of the gift of that office to Paul and Barnabas, through the laying on of hands. The laying on of hands in this case was merely confirming in the natural, that which the Holy Spirit had already done in the spirit. Unlike spiritual gifts, ministry gifts are not imparted through the laying on of hands. Ministry gifts are given directly from the Lord, as recorded in Ephesians chapter four (for more on this subject, see my book "Ministry Gifts").

Acts 14:23 "So when they had appointed elders in every church, and prayed with fasting, they commended them to the Lord in whom they had believed."

1 Timothy 3:1-8 "This is a faithful saying: If a man desires the position of a bishop, he desires a good work. (2) A bishop then must be blameless, the husband of one wife, temperate, sober-minded, of good behavior, hospitable, able to teach; ... (8) Likewise, deacons must be reverent, not double-tongued, not given to much wine, not greedy for money."

Acts 6:2-6 "Then the twelve summoned the multitude of the disciples and said, "It is not desirable that we should leave the word of God and serve tables. (3) Therefore, brethren, seek out from among you seven men of good reputation, full of the Holy Spirit and wisdom, whom we may appoint over this business; (4) but we will give ourselves continually to prayer and to the ministry of the word." (5) And the saying pleased the whole multitude. And they chose Stephen, a man full of faith and the Holy Spirit, and Philip, Prochorus, Nicanor, Timon, Parmenas, and Nicolas, a proselyte from Antioch, (6) whom they set before the apostles; and when they had prayed, they laid hands on them."

With the appointing of elders in the church, things work differently to the ministry gifts. Whereas ministry gifts are appointed by the Lord, elders are appointed by the Lord's ministry gifts. The elder in this instance, is not to be confused with the ministry gift of the pastor. For the office of pastor is one of the ministry gifts, and those called by the Lord to be a pastor, are appointed by Him. The Holy Spirit reveals to us in the portion of scripture from Acts chapter fourteen, that Paul and Barnabas would appoint elders in every church that they started. Before they appointed elders, they would first ensure that those elders met the requirements as taught by the Holy Spirit, in first Timothy chapter three. The word translated "bishop" in this passage of scripture, is the same word that is translated "elder" elsewhere. The scripture states that Paul and Barnabas would commend these elders to the Lord. They did so, by laying hands on them in front of the whole church, that were present as witnesses. In this instance, when Paul and Barnabas would lay hands on these elders, there would be an impartation of anointing that would take place. Which is one of the reasons that Paul and Barnabas prayed and fasted, before laying hands on the elders that they were inaugurating. Because these elders had not been separated by the Lord for ministry, they would not have an anointing on them, given to them directly from the Lord. Something similar would take place in this instance, as when Moses laid hands on Joshua. If you recall, we read earlier that at the Lord's instruction, Moses inaugurated Joshua into his office. When Moses inaugurated Joshua through the laying on of hands, he imparted to Joshua some of the authority and wisdom that he had in his ministry. In the same manner, elders are inaugurated into their offices by the ministry gifts. Paul and Barnabas would impart to the elders, part of their ministry anointing, so that they could operate in the office of elder. The primary anointing that is imparted through the ministry gifts to those appointed as elders, is the shepherds anointing. For elders are appointed as overseers of the local church, and their mandate is to shepherd the Lord's sheep. With the appointment of deacons in the church, things work in the same manner as the appointment of elders. The only difference is in the type of anointing that is imparted. As with elders, deacons must first meet the requirements as laid down in scripture by the Holy Spirit, in first Timothy chapter three. Those who meet these requirements, are then inaugurated into this office through the laying on of hands. Again, it is the ministry gifts that lay hands on the deacons, because they can impart of their anointing to the deacons to enable them to operate in that office. The primary anointing that is imparted through the ministry gifts to those appointed as deacons, is the anointing of helps, as recorded in first Corinthians chapter twelve. For deacons are appointed as helpers in the local church, and their mandate is to help in the day to day running of the church. Notice in the above passage of scripture from Acts chapter six, that even though these seven men were chosen by the church, it was still the ministry gifts of the apostles, that laid hands on them. For the Holy Spirit, has given the ministry gifts the ability to impart some of their anointing to the offices of elders and deacons. The impartation that takes place through the laying on of hands to inaugurate elders and deacons, is not an impartation of spiritual gifts. But rather it is an impartation of the ministry anointing required to stand in those offices.

Imparting blessing

Genesis 48:14-19 "Then Israel stretched out his right hand and laid it on Ephraim's head, who was the younger, and his left hand on Manasseh's head, guiding his hands knowingly, for Manasseh was the firstborn. (15) And he blessed Joseph, and said: "God, before whom my fathers Abraham and Isaac walked, The God who has fed me all my life long to this day, (16) The Angel who has redeemed me from all evil, Bless the lads; Let my name be named upon them, And the name of my fathers Abraham and Isaac; And let them grow into a multitude in the midst of the earth." (17) Now when Joseph saw that his father laid his right hand on the head of Ephraim, it displeased him; so he took hold of his father's hand to remove it from Ephraim's head to Manasseh's head. (18) And Joseph said to his father, "Not so, my father, for this one is the firstborn; put your right hand on his head." (19) But his father refused and said, "I know, my son, I know. He also shall become a people, and he also shall be great; but truly his younger brother shall be greater than he, and his descendants shall become a multitude of nations."

Hebrews 11:21 "By faith Jacob, when he was dying, blessed each of the sons of Joseph, and worshiped, leaning on the top of his staff."

There is one other area where we are taught to lay hands on people, and that is in the area of imparting the Lord's blessing to them. This is another aspect of ministry that was practiced under the Old Covenant and one which we also practice under the New Covenant. In the above account, we see Israel blessing Joseph's sons through prophecy, and the laying on of hands. That which Israel spoke over the lives of these young boys not only came to pass, but also affected whole peoples that were descended from them. And so, we see that this type of blessing can be extremely powerful. But it must be done in faith. We know that Israel blessed these young boys by faith, because scripture teaches us this fact (as quoted from the book of Hebrews above). As an aside, this scripture teaches us that the greater blessing comes through the right hand, rather than the left. We saw earlier when we looked at this scripture, that the gifts of the Spirit are not influenced by which hand is used. But it is very clear from this scripture, that blessing that is imparted through the laying on of hands, is affected by which hand is used. We see many instances in scripture, where the right hand of the Lord is mentioned in relation to His strength and His blessing. If God imparts His blessing through His right hand, then we should do the same.

Mark 10:13-16 "Then they brought little children to Him, that He might touch them; but the

Laying hands on believers

disciples rebuked those who brought them. (14) But when Jesus saw it, He was greatly displeased and said to them, "Let the little children come to Me, and do not forbid them; for of such is the kingdom of God. (15) Assuredly, I say to you, whoever does not receive the kingdom of God as a little child will by no means enter it." (16) And He took them up in His arms, laid His hands on them, and blessed them."

Hebrews 7:7 "Now beyond all contradiction the lesser is blessed by the better."

Luke 24:50-51 "And He led them out as far as Bethany, and He lifted up His hands and blessed them. (51) Now it came to pass, while He blessed them, that He was parted from them and carried up into heaven."

The New Testament only gives us two accounts, of the practice of imparting blessing, through the laying on of hands. And both were done by the Lord Jesus. In the above instance quoted from Mark's gospel, our Lord Jesus blessed the little children by laying His hands on them, and pronouncing a blessing on them. I have no doubt that our Lord prophesied blessings over these young lives, and that each one of His prophetic utterances came to pass in their lives. Our Lord would have done exactly what Israel did, by speaking a blessing over their lives, in faith. With regards to the ministry of blessing through the laying on of hands, it is subject to the spiritual law revealed to us in the book of Hebrews, quoted above. When the scripture speaks of the lesser being blessed by the better, it simply means that the one who is walking in the Lord's blessing can in turn impart that blessing to another who is not yet walking in that same degree of blessing. To give an example of how God views who is better and who is lesser, we can look at the example of Israel blessing Pharaoh, as recorded in Genesis chapter forty-seven. At the time, Jacob was the head of a nation of just seventy-five people. Because of the famine in the land, he was reliant on the generosity of Pharaoh, to sustain him and his family in Egypt. Pharaoh on the other hand, was the leader of the most powerful nation on the earth at that time, with all the wealth and prestige that went with his position. And yet the scripture tells us that when Israel stood before Pharaoh, that Jacob blessed Pharaoh. In God's eyes, Jacob was the better, and Pharaoh was the lesser. Parents and grandparents need to take note here. You have biblical authority to lay hands on your children and grandchildren, and by faith, pronounce blessings upon them. That which is spoken in faith, God will honour, and bring that to pass in their lives. Not always did the Lord physically lay His hands on people, in order to minister His blessing to them. In the above account from the book of Acts, our Lord raised His hands and blessed the disciples, without physically touching them. It is therefore scriptural in church meetings, when people are brought before the congregation for prayer, and those in leadership request that hands be stretched out in prayer to bless those in need. And so, we see that blessing can and should be imparted to people, through the laying on of hands.

Chapter 4
Transference of sin

Do not lay hands hastily

Leviticus 24:10-15 "Now the son of an Israelite woman, whose father was an Egyptian, went out among the children of Israel; and this Israelite woman's son and a man of Israel fought each other in the camp. (11) And the Israelite woman's son blasphemed the name of the LORD and cursed; and so they brought him to Moses. (His mother's name was Shelomith the daughter of Dibri, of the tribe of Dan.) (12) Then they put him in custody, that the mind of the LORD might be shown to them. (13) And the LORD spoke to Moses, saying, (14) "Take outside the camp him who has cursed; then let all who heard him lay their hands on his head, and let all the congregation stone him. (15) "Then you shall speak to the children of Israel, saying: 'Whoever curses his God shall bear his sin."

1 Timothy 5:19-24 "Do not receive an accusation against an elder except from two or three witnesses. (20) Those who are sinning rebuke in the presence of all, that the rest also may fear. (21) I charge you before God and the Lord Jesus Christ and the elect angels that you observe these things without prejudice, doing nothing with partiality. (22) Do not lay hands on anyone hastily, nor share in other people's sins; keep yourself pure. ... (24) Some men's sins are clearly evident, preceding them to judgment, but those of some men follow later."

Numbers 22:12-22 "And God said to Balaam, "You shall not go with them; you shall not curse the people, for they are blessed." ... (21) So Balaam rose in the morning, saddled his donkey, and went with the princes of Moab. (22) Then God's anger was aroused because he went, and the Angel of the LORD took His stand in the way as an adversary against him. And he was riding on his donkey, and his two servants were with him."

Events occurred in the Old Testament as examples for us to look at, and were recorded for our admonition. In the above recorded incident in Leviticus, we see God's judgement being pronounced on this individual, for the sin that he committed. But there is something else that we see in this incident, and that is the picture of contamination. Sin is as a virus, and if not dealt with, a virus can spread. This individual had sinned; in that he had blasphemed. But his blasphemy had been heard by others, and that had the effect of contaminating them with the same sin. To cleanse Israel from the sin virus that had manifested among them, the person, or carrier of the virus if you will, had to be destroyed. But at the same time the Lord had to decontaminate those who had been infected, so to speak. The Lord did that by having them lay their hands on the person who had committed the sin, and thus transferring the sin virus back to its originator. As we go through this section of the teaching on the laying on of hands, we will see the same principle being applied under the new covenant. In that we are to treat sin as a virus, that must be dealt with. Under the new covenant we no longer destroy the carrier of the virus, but rather we quarantine them from the rest of the body, so that the infection cannot spread to the rest of the body. In the passage of scripture quoted from first Timothy, the Holy Spirit through the apostle Paul, warns believers not to be hasty in laying hands on others. That warning seems to be in contradiction to what the bible teaches us about laying on of hands. In context, however, when the Holy Spirit warns us not to act hastily in laying hands on others, He is referring to laying hands on believers, and not unbelievers. And He is specifically speaking about sin in believers, affecting the person who is laying hands on them. For Paul warns Timothy not to share in other people's sins, but to keep himself pure. All unbelievers are full of sin, for scripture refers to them as sinners. And yet we are instructed in scripture, to lay hands on the unsaved. Sin in unbelievers, cannot affect believers who lay their hands on them. The reason for that is because we have been translated from the power of darkness into the kingdom of the Lord Jesus Christ. In Christ, the believer has power over the kingdom of darkness. And so, when we lay hands on unbelievers the only flow of anointing that takes place, is from our hands into their bodies, to destroy the works of the devil. There is no transference of any sin from the unbeliever to the believer. And so, the Holy Spirit is not warning us about sin in unbelievers affecting the one who is laying hands. He is referring to sin in believers, affecting fellow believers. So, what does that mean? In all instances the person doing the praying, is blessing the person being prayed for. A problem can arise however, if the person trying to bless the other through the laying on of hands, is going against God's will. What do I mean? Let's take healing as an example. It may be that the person being prayed for, has been judged by the

Lord with that sickness, because of unrepentant sin in their lives. For a believer to now lay hands on that person to bless them, would bring that believer into direct opposition to the Lord, and it may be that the Lord will now hold them accountable for that sin. In the above example given in the book of Numbers, this exact scenario took place, only in reverse. The prophet Balaam was trying to curse the children of Israel, even after the Lord had told him not to do so. Because the Lord had blessed them. Balaam stubbornly went ahead in trying to curse them, because of his love of money. For the people who hired him, had offered him great reward if he would curse Israel. In continuing to try and curse those whom God had blessed, Balaam found himself in direct opposition to the Lord, and it almost cost him his life. We all know the account of how Balaam's donkey saved him from the angel's sword and certain death. Again, this account was written for our instruction that it is not wise for us to go against God, in trying to curse those whom He has blessed. But in the same manner it is also not wise for us to go against God, in trying to bless those whom He has judged.

1 Corinthians 5:6-13 "Your glorying is not good. Do you not know that a little leaven leavens the whole lump? (7) Therefore purge out the old leaven, that you may be a new lump, since you truly are unleavened. For indeed Christ, our Passover, was sacrificed for us. ... (11) But now I have written to you not to keep company with anyone named a brother, who is sexually immoral, or covetous, or an idolater, or a reviler, or a drunkard, or an extortioner--not even to eat with such a person. (12) For what have I to do with judging those also who are outside? Do you not judge those who are inside? (13) But those who are outside God judges. Therefore "PUT AWAY FROM YOURSELVES THE EVIL PERSON."

2 John 1:9-11 "Whoever transgresses and does not abide in the doctrine of Christ does not have God. He who abides in the doctrine of Christ has both the Father and the Son. (10) If anyone comes to you and does not bring this doctrine, do not receive him into your house nor greet him; (11) for he who greets him shares in his evil deeds."

In the passage of scripture quoted from second John, the Holy Spirit through the apostle John, warns the believer not to invite certain people into their homes, or to even greet them. In context, the people the Holy Spirit is referring to, are those who are knowingly preaching false doctrine. The Lord tells us that if we go ahead and invite these people into our homes or even greet them, then we have become partakers in their evil deeds. To share in their deeds, implies that we will incur the same judgement that our Lord has pronounced on these individuals. Therefore, how much more won't the believer be judged, who then lays hands on people such as these, to try and bless them. We should not be naïve but rather be aware, regarding the people we lay hands on. The Holy Spirit teaches us in first Corinthians quoted above, that a little leaven leavens the whole lump. He is specifically talking about sin in believers, being able to impact the lives of other believers. The reason that can happen, is because we are all from the same lump, as we are all part of the body of Christ. Unbelievers are not part of our lump so to speak, and therefore their sin cannot affect us. Notice that the Holy Spirit counsels us to cut ties with these believers, to not even share a meal with them. The reason He says this, is because sin can be likened to a virus. And that virus can spread in the body, unless it is quarantined. I have experienced an incident along this line. A while ago I was at a breakfast meeting, and we were praying around the table for various things. There was someone at our table that I had never met before, and this person had been introduced to me as a brother in the Lord. Someone at our table asked me to pray for this person to just bless them. I agreed and bowed my head to pray, but nothing came out. It was as if there was a hold on my tongue. There was silence around the table as everyone waited for me to pray, but try as I might, I could not pray. Eventually, when it started to get a bit embarrassing because of the silence, I managed to just ask the Lord to reveal His will to this person, and quickly closed my prayer on that point. I later found out that this person was living as a homosexual. I realized then, just why the Holy Spirit would not allow me to pray for this individual, to bless them. Because, if I had tried to bless them, I would have been praying contrary to the will of God. We are not to lay hands hastily on anyone.

If you believe you can receive Jesus as your Lord and Saviour by praying this prayer

Dear Heavenly Father,

I come to You in the Name of Jesus.

Your Word says, "the one who comes to Me I will by no means cast out" (John 6:37), so I know You won't cast me out, but You take me in and I thank You for it. You said in Your Word, "Whoever calls on the name of the lord shall be saved." (Romans 10:13). I am calling on Your Name, so I know that You save me right now. You also said, "If you confess with your mouth the Lord Jesus and believe in your heart that God has raised Him from the dead, you will be saved. (10) For with the heart one believes unto righteousness, and with the mouth confession is made unto salvation" (Romans 10:9-10). I believe in my heart Jesus Christ is the Son of God. I believe that He was raised from the dead for my justification, and I confess Him now as my Lord. Because Your Word says, "with the heart one believes unto righteousness," and I do believe with my heart, I have now become the righteousness of God in Christ Jesus (2 Cor. 5:21) . . .

And I am now saved!

Thank You, Lord!

Welcome to the family of God. Now that you are His child you need to read your bible (especially the New

Testament) daily, spend time in prayer daily and join a local church that will teach you to be filled with the Holy Spirit with the evidence of speaking in other tongues, so that you can grow spiritually. You also need to tell others how Jesus has saved you so that they too can be saved.

About the Author

From childhood, Michael E.B. Maher has always known that the Lord's call was upon his life for the ministry. When he was saved at the age of twenty-two, almost immediately the Lord Jesus began to deal with him about entering the ministry. He went to Oral Roberts University to enrol but circumstances prevented him from following that path. After a period, the call for the ministry once again became very strong, and finally in the early 1990's Michael entered the ministry. After a period, he left the ministry and went into the business world. Although he experienced success in the business world, he was outside of the Lord's will for his life. Over time, he began to drift from the close relationship with the Lord that he had always known. By 2010 the Lord's patience had run out, and Michael suffered his first series of heart attacks. By this time, Michael had become so worldly in his thinking that it never even occurred to him that the Lord had begun to judge him for his disobedience. After his medical treatment, Michael went back into his career thinking that all was back on track again. But now the Lord started to unravel his career as well. Whereas before he had always excelled in his work, he now found completely dissatisfied with what he was doing. And so, at the height of his career he decided to take early retirement. It was during this time that his relationship with the Lord grew again. Although the Lord had brought him to this point, he was still not in the Lord's will. And so, Michael then had his next series of heart attacks. It was only now that the Lord finally got his attention and he committed to the Lord that if He would spare his life, that he would finally answer the Lord's call to the ministry.

And so, in 2014 Michael Maher Ministries was begun. From the beginning, the mandate given to Michael from the Lord Jesus was to preach the word. And so, this ministry preaches the word of God on every available platform around the world.

Michael Maher Ministries

Free Subscription

Join hundreds of others from countries around the world
and read our Daily Bible Teaching Email and more, that
will help you to grow in your walk with the Lord Jesus.

*Thank you so much for your dedication and
commitment. These daily teachings are invaluable to me
and my family.*
Kind regards
Bill

-    *Bill Watt-Pringle*

Hi Michael
*Thanx so much for this word, it really struck home. It's
now helping me to get my act together*
Sue

-    *Suzanne Honeyborne*

*Thank u for explaining. Your messages are very helpful
to keep reading & renewing my mind*

-    *Alison Joy Kruger Hale*

Log on to our website to subscribe.

www.mebmm.org

Michael Maher Ministries

Online Bible Courses

Our courses are designed to help believers grow in their faith and reach their full potential in Christ that God intended for their lives, through the study of His word.

Flexible

Enrol any time: choose your topic of study; study at your own pace.

Affordable

Pay as you go.

Log on to our website to register.

www.mebmm.org

Michael Maher Ministries

13 Windsor Lodge
Beach Road
Fish Hoek, 7974
Cape Town
South Africa
Phone: +27 082-974-3599

On the Web

www.mebmm.org